SIGNAL SUCCESS IN BRIDGE

Players are generally aware of the fact that accurate signalling plays a key role in conducting a successful defence. In tournament bridge, especially, it is vital for the defenders to extract every ounce of value from the dismal cards they have at their disposal. This book tells you how to do it.

Those who think they know all about signalling will be surprised to discover how much they still have to learn. In a comprehensive survey, the author covers every aspect of this difficult subject, introducing you to signals that you may not have imagined in your wildest dreams. You may decide in the end that some of the subtler methods are not for you, but you will surely be stimulated by many of the ideas. A careful study of this book will do a lot to help your defence.

Danny Roth scored a palpable hit with his first book, *Clues to Winning Play*. This, his second effort, will enhance his reputation as a new writer of power and authority.

Also by Danny Roth

CLUES TO WINNING PLAY:
Detective Work in Bridge

Signal Success in Bridge

DANNY ROTH

VICTOR GOLLANCZ LTD
in association with
Peter Crawley
1989

First published in Great Britain 1989
in association with Peter Crawley
by Victor Gollancz Ltd
14 Henrietta Street, London WC2E 8QJ

British Library Cataloguing in Publication Data
Roth, Danny
    Signal success in bridge.—(Master bridge series).
    1. Contract bridge. Card play by defenders—Manuals
    I. Title   II. Series
    795.41'53

ISBN 0-575-04571-X

Photoset by Rowland Phototypesetting Ltd
Bury St Edmunds, Suffolk
Printed in Great Britain by
St Edmundsbury Press Ltd, Bury St Edmunds, Suffolk

Contents

1. Setting the Scene

The world's worst card-holder? Yes, everybody knows—it's you!

Let us face it—if you don't get any cards, you are going to have to learn to defend.

Even the average card-holder, on whom you look with such passionate envy, has little over which to get excited. The most common hand pattern is 4 4 3 2, so something like:

♠ A 9 7 3; ♡ Q 4; ◇ J 8 6 2; ♣ K 10 5—a perfectly fair share of aces, kings etc. adding up to a boring ten count.

Furthermore, with the laws as they stand, even the average card-holder will, on average, play one hand for every two he defends unless his style of bidding is very selfish and/or competitive.

The purpose of this book is to help improve partnership cooperation in defence and to illustrate that it can be the most satisfying aspect of the game. After all, any fool can bid 7NT and claim on a 37 count. The expert is one who can win irrespective of what he is dealt or the form of scoring. Here, we shall be concerned primarily with rubber bridge or team (IMP) scoring where the prime object is to defeat the contract. The additional considerations of pairs must be left for the moment.

It is generally accepted that defence is the most difficult part of the game. A sound knowledge of your system combined with a reasonable level of commonsense judgment will keep your bidding to a reasonable standard even in top-class company. On the playing side, declarer has a number of advantages:

a) Except in very low-level contracts or sacrifice situations, he holds the balance of power and therefore is likely to have more control over the timing of the play.
b) He has the facility to play as deceptively as he wishes without risk of fooling his partner who takes no part in the proceedings.
c) As he operates both hands, he can arrange that his hand and dummy's play in perfect cohesion, whereas the defenders

may find themselves at cross-purposes if they take different views of a situation.

d) He knows exactly the total forces in his favour and which cards are against him.

e) The defence includes the opening lead which has to be made with only thirteen cards on view.

Clearly, therefore, the defenders have the more difficult task . . . or have they? Because if they have, there is a little mystery. Before reading on, can you think of two good arguments which heavily counterbalance the points above?

Firstly, there is the obvious factor of practice. As was explained earlier, you will defend two hands for every one you play.

Secondly, and a point very often missed, the defender usually has more information than his adversary. The declarer, particularly in high-level contracts where mistakes are most expensive, will often have bid against silent opposition. Thus, while he knows what he is up against, he has little idea of where the enemy weapons are. The defender, however, can also see twenty-six cards and he, one hundred times out of one hundred, will have opponents' bidding to help him place the remainder. This particularly applies nowadays with so many highly sophisticated systems in vogue. Several experts have devised sequences by which large numbers of bids are made with a view to expressing length and strength very accurately. Such systems carry the inevitable disadvantage of making defence that much easier and are thus arguably dubious assets.

The mystery?—as an avid collector of bridge mistakes, your author has found that he makes at least three times as many mistakes as a declarer than as a defender and there is certainly no claim to defensive brilliance. If any aptitude can be claimed, it is in card-reading and that is easier for the defender. Card-reading was at the heart of the first book *Clues to Winning Play* and will be again here. Defensive signalling is an aid to good card-reading: it is very easy to play when you can see all four hands—the aim is to help you 'see' all four hands . . . legally!

To get everything together, much research has been done through masses of books, match reports and magazine articles and the following conclusions are apparent:

1) Situations in bridge are so variable that, if you are going to be consistently successful in defence, you must be very flexible. Thus, strict adherence to hard and fast rules simply is not good enough. Rules, it has been said, are for the obedience of fools and for the guidance of wise men. They must be considered as guides to be followed with discretion and no more.
2) At the lower levels of bridge, by far the majority of defensive mistakes are caused by what might be called 'lack of awareness': not knowing where certain cards are when one should have known.
3) In stronger company, a large proportion of defensive disasters seem to be due to a failure to use suit-preference signals.
4) A considerable proportion of hands, even those where difficult defences are involved, call for no defensive signalling at all. It is, therefore, necessary to recognise situations in which signals are required otherwise there is a danger of attaching a meaning to every card—signal mania, as the disease might be called—putting an intolerable strain on the partnership.

Readers may appreciate from the above comments that it might well be that one of the prime reasons for the very low overall standard of defence lies in the way bridge is taught. Before going further, it should be stressed that no word should be heard against any bridge school or teacher as most of them display patience and kindness worthy of canonisation. But as their aim is to teach their pupils enough, in a limited time, to enable them to join in and enjoy a game (which is, after all, the object of the exercise) they tend to lead them up potentially hazardous paths. Once habits are started, they can be very difficult to break.

How often have we all heard the rules?

1) Against no-trumps, lead the fourth highest of your best, usually longest, suit.
2) Second hand plays low.
3) Third hand plays high.
4) Prefer to lead from solid sequences (e.g. K Q J) than from broken ones (e.g. A Q 10).
5) Aim to lead through strength on your left and round to weakness on your right.

6) Never discard so as to leave a king unguarded or from holdings like queen to three. . . .

and so the list goes on.

They are all very sensible but the number of times that one has to break the above rules is so great that they are of limited value—at least without a full understanding of why they exist. It is only this understanding that permits the knowledge of when they should be broken and that is the key to good defence.

The first step towards good card-reading is what might be called 'The Seven Roll-Calls'. Basically, they concern the above parameters measured in closer detail:

The distribution round the table of:

1) Spades
2) Hearts
3) Diamonds
4) Clubs
5) High card points

and from them

6) How many tricks are available on top (or are easily establishable) to declarer?
7) How many such tricks are available to the defenders?

Yes, it is hard work but that is defence! To have to ask yourself and answer all these questions hand after hand, often several times during one board, is likely to leave you shattered at the end of an evening of poor cards. Few people seem to realise that, if you want success, you have got to work for it.

Let us look at our prime tools in more detail: the first point to note is their close interconnection. Once dummy goes down, you can see twenty-six cards and the problem is to place the remainder. Once you know the count of one of the unseen hands in three suits, you automatically know the count of the fourth. Even if you only know about two, the bidding should at least give you a rough guide to the others. All that is involved is adding up to thirteen four times.

Proceeding to points, you note that there are forty in the pack.

Thus, by adding your meagre allocation to dummy's and deducting the answer from that total, you have the combined strength of partner and declarer. The bidding should give some indication of declarer's point count and the rest must be with partner. Points and distribution also have their link. For example, if the bidding marks declarer (South) with a void of spades, he cannot have any points in that suit and therefore any points he does hold must be elsewhere. If it is clear that he has a singleton, he cannot have more than four points in the suit; a doubleton implies a maximum of seven and so on.

It all seems a statement of the obvious but the number of people, including many who have represented their nation, who do not seem to be aware of this, is disturbingly high.

Having covered points and distribution, we can now proceed to tricks: for and against. The number of cards in each suit in declarer's and dummy's hands will give us a guide as to how many rounds of the suit are likely to be played. We then consider potential winners and losers and finish with a full picture of our prospects. Again note the interconnection. The more high cards in a suit held by a partnership, the more tricks they are likely to take. With trumps, there is the additional point that, if conditions permit, tricks may be won separately.

If only you are prepared to make the effort, it is amazing what you can find out! Just ask yourself the questions and answer them. If your answers are consistent with the bidding and play so far, assume they are correct; if not, try again.

The best way to tackle your seven roll-calls is to start with those where the answers are obvious and to work towards those where you haven't got a clue. Here is a simple example where you are West. You will have to be on your toes and do your roll-calls at trick one so that you are not caught in that all too informative trance:

Hand No. 1
Dealer South
N–S Vulnerable

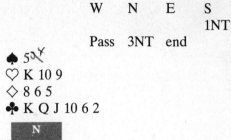

W	N	E	S
			1NT
Pass	3NT	end	

♠ 5 Q X
♡ K 10 9
◇ 8 6 5
♣ K Q J 10 6 2

♠ Q J 10 7
♡ A 7 5 2
◇ A Q
♣ 7 5 4

South's opener showed 12–14. You lead the queen of spades to the five, partner's two and declarer's ace. You have agreed to play encouraging/discouraging signals on trick one. South now leads the jack of hearts; plan your defence.

Let's do the seven roll-calls and see what we can find out: with no suits having been bid, we know little about the suit distribution but we do know quite a bit about points. There are 13 in the West hand and 9 in dummy leaving 18 unaccounted for. The bidding suggests South has around 13 leaving partner with about 5. Let us now consider tricks. You can see that North has made something of a gamble on his low point count so the club suit will have to come in if this contract is going to make. South can play up to six rounds if he wishes, making five or six tricks according to who has the ace. You will surely agree that, if South did not have the ace, the first thing he would have done is to knock it out, particularly as dummy is short of entries. As he didn't, he clearly has it himself. We can now do our points roll-call in more detail. Partner's discouragement of the spades indicates that he has neither ace nor king; therefore they must be with South. Added to the club ace, this gives 11 points so far. The jack of hearts makes it up to 12 and therefore he cannot have the king of diamonds. Returning to the number of tricks, we see that there are 6 in clubs, 2 in spades and none in diamonds so declarer needs 1 in hearts and is clearly trying to steal it now before you realise that he is wide open in diamonds. You must, therefore, rise with the ace and bang down the ace and queen of diamonds hoping that partner can take four tricks in the suit.

The deal:

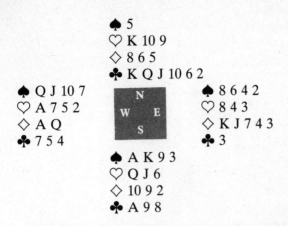

♠ 5
♥ K 10 9
♦ 8 6 5
♣ K Q J 10 6 2

♠ Q J 10 7   ♠ 8 6 4 2
♥ A 7 5 2   ♥ 8 4 3
♦ A Q   ♦ K J 7 4 3
♣ 7 5 4   ♣ 3

♠ A K 9 3
♥ Q J 6
♦ 10 9 2
♣ A 9 8

You can see how your partner's two of spades helped with your points roll-call. In the following chapters, we shall see how other signals can help pinpoint outstanding important cards. But so much for 'Second hand plays low' and 'Don't lead away from holdings like A Q'.

This hand was included to illustrate how dangerous it can be to adhere to 'general rules'. No beginner would have had a chance to defeat this contract and one wonders how many recognised experts would have allowed South to get away with such daylight robbery simply by failing to ask themselves the 'Magic Question' which was introduced in *Clues to Winning Play*.

It is: 'What on Earth is going on here?' and the importance of it cannot really be emphasised too often.

In the above hand, South was trying to steal his ninth trick by giving the impression that he was taking a finesse against the queen of hearts. Deception is a very important part of play and defence and we shall be looking at it in more detail later on.

Meanwhile, try another hand from the East seat:

Hand No. 2

Dealer South
N–S Vulnerable

W	N	E	S
			1NT
Pass	2♣	Pass	2◇
Pass	2NT	Pass	3NT
end			

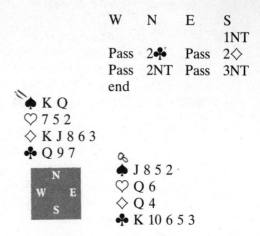

♠ K Q
♡ 7 5 2
◇ K J 8 6 3
♣ Q 9 7

♠ J 8 5 2
♡ Q 6
◇ Q 4
♣ K 10 6 5 3

South's opener showed 13–15. North had to go through Stayman to invite game as a direct 2NT would have been Baron showing 16+ points with slam ambitions.

West leads the four of hearts, playing fourth-high leads. Dummy plays the deuce, you the queen and South the ace. He continues with the four of spades to partner's six and dummy's king. Now, please think very carefully about this—which card are you going to play? It will be a pleasant surprise if one reader in a thousand is able to give me the correct answer with logical reasons.

Well, you had four choices. You probably will be surprised to learn that you can play the two or five or eight or jack with complete impunity as it is of no relevance to the defence of this hand whatsoever. Perhaps you played the five or eight in order to give your partner a count on the suit. But he knows it already. South denied four spades and must therefore have exactly two or three to have opened 1NT. With two, he certainly wouldn't have touched the suit, not to mention that partner would have surely led it with a five-card, so he has exactly three and both E–W know the other has four. Roll-calling the spade suit further, we know that South's three spades are A x x. He would not have touched the suit otherwise. Thus the spade situation is clearly known and which card you play couldn't matter less.

Then why was such a silly question asked in a book on defensive signalling? Primarily, it is an attempt to emphasise the importance of knowing when signals apply and just as important, when they do not. When South played that spade, did you ask yourself why or just pick a card to follow thinking no more of it? The question applies because, despite the irrelevance of your choice of card, this was the most important trick of the play. If the penny still hasn't dropped, let us digress from bridge for a moment in favour of the world of the riddle.

Question: Why did the chicken cross the road?
Answer: To get to the other side.

You can see that South has three spade tricks, no more, no less so the only purpose of playing that spade was to get to dummy. Have you seen the light now? If not, think further. What is he going to do when he gets there? We have roll-called the spade suit in detail but now let's look at declarer's tricks. With the awful spade duplication, it is clear that the diamond suit will have to be brought in; so South is intending to play it from the table. That's bad news; you were hoping he would play it from hand and run the jack to your queen. This implies that, if South has the ace of diamonds, the finesse will work and the contract will almost certainly make but . . . let's roll-call the points. We know from the bidding that South has 14–15 and the play so far accounts for the two major aces. We also noted that he won the first trick when he could have ducked, which strongly suggests he has the king of hearts as well and possibly the ten in addition. That is why he wanted to play the diamond finesse that way—to protect the heart holding. But what finesse? With eleven points known, he could have the diamond ace but it may be a Chinese finesse situation—an attempt to lose the first diamond trick to West. You will have to rise with the queen of diamonds to keep partner's entry intact. In other words, the layout you have to cope with is this:

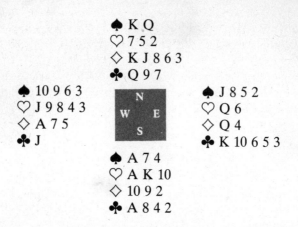

```
                    ♠ K Q
                    ♡ 7 5 2
                    ◇ K J 8 6 3
                    ♣ Q 9 7
  ♠ 10 9 6 3           N           ♠ J 8 5 2
  ♡ J 9 8 4 3    W         E       ♡ Q 6
  ◇ A 7 5             S             ◇ Q 4
  ♣ J                               ♣ K 10 6 5 3
                    ♠ A 7 4
                    ♡ A K 10
                    ◇ 10 9 2
                    ♣ A 8 4 2
```

Failure to go up with the queen of diamonds reveals the position whether West wins or not and now the contract must make. But suppose the question had been phrased differently:

'. . . Partner leads the four of hearts to the two, queen and ace. South crosses to the king of spades and leads a low diamond from dummy; plan your defence.'

You then would probably have realised that this was your big moment and might well have come up with the right answer. But did you really appreciate what was happening when trick three was not specifically pinpointed as the crucial trick?

As was explained in the first book, this method of presentation of problems differs from those generally given and you may well agree that it is more realistic. In a match, you have no-one to tap you on the shoulder to tell you when that extra mental effort is required. You will also have noticed that the signals in this hand came from South rather than from partner.

Note also that it was not necessary to do all seven roll-calls on these two hands but rather to choose the important ones until you had enough information to conduct the defence sensibly. There will be hands, however, where all seven will be needed. The basic guide is not to play until you have a reasonable assumption of how the unseen cards are placed.

Before we go into the various types of signal, a couple of points regarding basic principles are in order.

Firstly, a signal should be considered as giving information to help partner with his seven roll-calls and for no other purpose.

No signal should be considered a command or even a suggestion. Thus, if you were to lead a winning heart and partner played an encouraging card, that does not mean:

'Partner, lead another one or play with someone else.' or

'Partner, you seem to have hit the right suit; might I humbly suggest that you give your consideration to the possibility of continuing the suit?'

or any of the dozen or so degrees of dogmatism between those two extremes. It is suggested that it should mean:

'Partner, I am interested in this suit; kindly take this into account when doing your seven roll-calls and defend accordingly.'

It has been emphasised many times that the crucial issue is: 'What, if anything, does partner need to know?'

There are a number of basic headings:

a) Encouragement or discouragement of the suit played.
b) Distribution of the suit played.
c) Suit preference.
d) Other vital information, including honour combinations, distribution of other suits, ruffing potential, location of specific vital cards.

The above factors are placed in that order because it is suggested that this is the order in which the defender's thoughts should run. Many players take a different view, believing that distribution should be the first priority. Whatever the order, it is important to choose the right one.

Accurate exchange of information requires the two defenders to be on the same wavelength and working hard on their roll-calls. Let us split up defence into a number of stages:

a) The opening lead: clues from the auction.
b) The play by East to trick one (you are West).
c) The information gained from the four cards played to trick one.
d) The early play and unveiling of declarer's plan if not already obvious.
e) The middle game—more information revealed.
f) The end-game when the hand will usually be an open book.

17

The vast majority of contracts are won or lost by the end of trick two. Sadly, that means that vital decisions have to be made when the least is known: such is life. Defenders must, therefore, ensure that they understand the bidding thoroughly, including negative inferences, before a card is played. In particular, if you are playing against people whose system is strange, make doubly sure that every ounce of information exchanged is in your possession. If they fail to give such information fully, they are, by the laws (and common sense for that matter), cheating. Insist on full disclosure, establishing what has been denied as well as what has been promised.

There are a number of considerations regarding the opening lead:

a) Active or passive? Has the bidding suggested that they are going to make their contract with tricks to spare or have they struggled into it? The relevant roll-calls are 6 and 7. How many easy tricks will be available to each side and what is their total? If it is thirteen or more, then a race is on and you must get busy even at the risk of giving away unnecessary tricks (probably overtricks of minimal value anyway). If the total is less than thirteen, then it is important not to give anything away and let declarer do his own work.

b) In the light of a), which suit should be led?

c) Once the suit is chosen, which card?

We shall look at a number of signalling systems with their advantages and disadvantages. The system played in my circle will then be set out and you will be invited to solve a number of defensive problems using it. You will be expected to recognise whether a signal is required and if so, when, and which defender should send the message and which should receive. There will, of course, be a few red herrings where no signalling is required.

2. Opening Lead Systems

A job well begun
Is a job half done!

It should be emphasised from the start that, in any discussion on the relative merits of various defensive signalling systems, one has to weigh up the advantage of giving more information to partner against the disadvantage of giving extra assistance to declarer. This should be borne in mind when considering the chapters that follow.

Let us assume that we have paid due attention to the bidding, have ensured that we understand it fully and have decided which suit to lead—it is now a question of which card.

The principal problem areas might be summarised as follows:

a) Honour combinations, notably A K.
b) Three small cards.
c) Longer suits of small cards.
d) Three cards including one honour.
e) Longer suits including an honour.
f) Whether a ten is to be considered as an honour.

We shall now look at a number of systems in the light of the above considerations:

STANDARD LEADS
Although there may be some variation, this usually means the top card from a sequence of honours: A from A K, K from K Q etc. and top from an internal sequence: J from K J 10, 10 from Q 10 9 etc. Many pairs, notably in America, prefer to lead the king from A K. The relative merits of the ace or king from ace, king and others have been argued for years and the two sides are as follows:

If you lead the ace, you automatically lose the facility to lead an ace and deny the king; this can be vital in quick cash-out situations.

However, if you lead the king from both A K and K Q, you will often leave scope for ambiguity. This layout would give East a problem:

$$8\ 5\ 2$$

K led   J 7 4

?

What is East to do? If the lead comes from A K, he will want to discourage lest South holds the queen, while if it comes from K Q, he will want to encourage to knock out South's ace and set up defensive tricks. Also, give East 7 4 doubleton against a trump contract and he is in more trouble. If West has the ace, East will want to peter to invite a third round ruff but if South has it, encouragement may result in his ducking and partner leading a second round to declarer's A J.

A further disadvantage of the lead of the king arises in suit contracts where partner is likely to be void. Arguably, he shouldn't ruff anyway as he will probably be ruffing a loser but if you have a good hand, he may think he can get two or more ruffs as you will have quick entries available. In that event, it is suggested that the ace should be led even if the partnership has agreed on the king in principle—best for keeping the peace!

The recommendation? You guessed it—be flexible! Lead ace from A K in principle except in obvious cash-out situations, notably where there are solid suits around. In these cases, lead the king, particularly if it is clear that layouts where ambiguity may occur are unlikely.

Mention of 'A K' implies 'A K and at least one other card'. Where you have a doubleton, you should cash your tricks 'the wrong way round' in any of the following situations:

a) You consider it vital to give partner the count.
b) You want to ruff the third round and believe there is a good chance that partner can get in before trumps are drawn.
c) You are intending to switch to a singleton in another suit; here you cash one honour only.
d) You have a vital suit-preference message to send.

TREBLETONS

With three small cards, there is a difference of opinion and this will have to be discussed in some detail. A case can be made for any of the three cards:

a) Top of nothing. There are two purposes:
   To tell partner you have no strength in the suit,
   To make at least a token attempt to hold the lead as here:

$$K\ 8\ 3$$

$$9\ 6\ 2 \qquad\qquad A\ Q\ J\ 10\ 4$$

$$7\ 5$$

Unless the nine is led, dummy can play low and the king, at least for the time being, is protected—could be important at no-trumps or in a forcing game at a suit contract.

   The disadvantage of top of nothing lies in its indistinguishability from the doubleton as, in virtually all systems, the top card is led from that holding. Thus, if East holds two quick tricks, he may be faced with a horrible decision here:

$$8\ 7$$

$$9\ \text{followed by}\ 6 \qquad\qquad A\ K\ Q\ 5\ 4\ 2$$

$$J\ 10\ 3$$

This is a side suit in a trump contract.

   On the first two rounds, South loses nothing by following with the jack and ten and if dummy's trumps are low, there may be a chance for a trump trick if East leads a third round. But put the trey into the West hand and the defence gives a ruff and discard.

b) Middle, Up, Down: This is affectionately known as MUD by its adherents and is an attempt to counter the disadvantages of the other two possibilities. Playing a card followed by a higher card promises a third card at least and thus rules out the doubleton. Equally, the size of the spots may clarify that there is no honour and thus distinguishes from three to an honour from which the lowest card is the standard lead.

   A number of top-class players have expressed strong views against the MUD lead. It has been pointed out that if East has two quick tricks in the suit he will not know that you have a trebleton until the second round and then it may be too late.

   One wonders whether anyone has gone into the pros and

cons of the MUD lead in anywhere near sufficient detail. In particular, nobody seems to have pointed out that a great deal depends on two factors:

i) The message you wish to send to partner.

ii) The size of your middle card.

It is one thing to lead the 8 from 9 8 4 but quite another to lead the 3 from 7 3 2 and yet both are MUD leads. If East is going to be misled, he will probably be looking for a doubleton in the first case and for an honour in the second. We must consider what East's holding is likely to be, what he might be able to see in dummy, South's likely holding on the bidding and the consequences of partner misreading your lead.

c) The lowest card to be followed by the highest then the middle. This is widely used in America and has been adopted here by many expert pairs having been described by a number of world class players as 'undoubtedly the best'.

The major advantages are:

i) That East can recognise a high spot card as coming from a singleton or doubleton most easily.

ii) South may be deceived into thinking that West has length and/or strength in the suit.

The disadvantages, however, may be considerable:

i) East may have problems in recognising low doubletons or singletons.

ii) The system involves leading the 2 from 7 3 2 and also from K J 8 2 or (playing 3rd and 5th leads), K J 8 5 2. If defenders want to treat such diverse holdings in a similar manner, then surely they will, from time to time at least, run into ambiguities. It certainly doesn't help the points roll-call.

To be fair, this is the only realistic way to rule out the doubleton at trick one but this is only likely to be important if East holds two quick tricks and even then the MUD lead can have the advantage.

Consider this hand:

Hand No. 3
Dealer North
Game All

	W	N	E	S
		1♣	1♢	2♠
	Pass	3♠	Pass	4♠
	end			

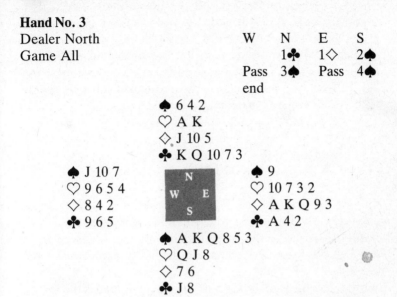

```
              ♠ 6 4 2
              ♡ A K
              ♢ J 10 5
              ♣ K Q 10 7 3
♠ J 10 7              N          ♠ 9
♡ 9 6 5 4         W      E       ♡ 10 7 3 2
♢ 8 4 2              S           ♢ A K Q 9 3
♣ 9 6 5                          ♣ A 4 2
              ♠ A K Q 8 5 3
              ♡ Q J 8
              ♢ 7 6
              ♣ J 8
```

West leads the four of diamonds and East cashes the queen and
king, West following with the TWO on the second round. Now
comes the ace of diamonds and would you like to be South? The
chances are he will ruff high and hope for a 2–2 trump split. He
thus goes off in a stone cold contract. The MUD lead retained a
deceptive option; the two of diamonds settles for −620 immediately.

Thus, it will be seen that there are advantages and disadvantages in any of the three possible leads and therefore the
recommendation should surely be: yes, you guessed it again—be
flexible. Why have a rule at all when it stands to gain little?
Roll-call the hand from the bidding, decide what information is
most important and which card is best suited to give that
information bearing in mind the card you intend to play to the
second round if there is likely to be one.

With longer suits of small cards again you must consider
whether length or strength should take priority. If it is length,
follow the standard procedure of leading the fourth highest
intending to follow with the fifth and lower cards if appropriate.
If you wish to warn your partner that you have no strength in the

suit, then the choice lies between the top and second highest. The crucial factor is whether you can afford that top card. The recommendation is that if your top two cards are in sequence, lead the higher i.e. 9 from 9 8 4 2 or 8 from 8 7 6 3. If they are not, then it might be best to draw the line around the eight spot: lead the 7 from 9 7 5 4 but also the 7 from 7 5 3 2 or the 6 from 6 4 3 2. With the 8 as highest card, you will have to decide whether the 8 is likely to be important as here:

$$5\ 4$$

$$8\ 6\ 3\ 2 \qquad\qquad Q\ 10\ 9$$

$$A\ K\ J\ 7$$

You might break the rules if you consider it vital to show weakness in the suit where your second card is deceptively low, notably if there is a switch you badly want. e.g. lead 9 from 9 4 3 2. Note again the accent on flexibility according to the situation.

With three cards to an honour, the standard lead is the lowest card which, according to the attitude principle (the lower the card the stronger my interest in the suit) shows some feature and a willingness to have the suit returned towards your hand.

With four-card or longer suits to one or more honours, the standard lead is the fourth highest. This should not be higher than the eight spot otherwise you will have an honour combination.

Partner (but note also declarer) may now use the rule of eleven to determine the number of cards higher than the card led which are still outstanding. In variations discussed below, if you prefer to lead third highest from long suits, you use the rule of twelve, with fifth highest, the rule of ten, fifteen being the pivotal total.

There are two disadvantages of fourth-high leads.
i) They do not necessarily give the exact length which may be important in cash-out situations.
ii) It may be difficult to distinguish between three and four to an honour.

The final point to consider in the above list is the status of the ten. It is a generally accepted practice in all leading systems to treat the ten as an honour and where it can help set up tricks for other honours, this would seem reasonable. However, where opponents dominate the suit, the other view is likely to be preferable. Again, you must consider the three basic points:

i) Whether you want a switch.
ii) Do you want to indicate count or attitude?
iii) Can you afford the ten?

Flexibility must again prevail.

Before moving on to more modern leading systems, one variation from standard practice, which has proved useful without introducing any confusion, might be mentioned. That is to lead the queen from A K Q. This has never led to a mishap and affords the facility to lead the ace from A K and automatically deny the queen; a great help for the points roll-call. Similarly, we lead the jack from A K Q J etc.

BLUE CLUB LEADS

Introduced by the Italian Blue team (and who can argue with their success?), these aim for greater clarity in honour leads as follows:

Ace: This requests partner to give distribution when following.

King: Guarantees at least three of the top five honours and usually coming from a long suit, requests partner to unblock.

Queen: From any of the following: A Q J x, K Q x x, Q J 10 x, Q J 9 x, and invites partner to overtake if possible and return the suit.

Jack: Promises a weak holding, typically Q J x x, J 10 9 x, J 10 x x.

Ten: Promises a strong holding with one of the top three honours and possibly the jack in addition, typically A J 10 x, K J 10 x, A 10 9 x, K 10 9 x, Q 10 9 x.

The nine must be led from 10 9 x.

There are obvious advantages over the standard lead system:

i) The jack indicates weakness categorically here, whereas before it could come from J 10 x x or K J 10 x x.
ii) East has clear instructions as to how to follow suit so mishaps caused by misunderstandings are unlikely.

However, there are disadvantages:

i) The system implies that West is in charge of the proceedings whereas, in many cases, East should be taking the decisions. We shall discuss this point in more detail later under the heading of 'the Captain's privilege'.

ii) There is a drawback in any leading system in which (except king from A K), the lead of an honour promises or implies possession of the honour immediately above it. So often you will want to lead an honour as a singleton or from a doubleton, for example Q x. East may misread the position completely, at least in respect of his points roll-call. Very often it should be possible to distinguish between short suit leads of this kind and the systemic lead but it is likely that disasters will occur in suit contracts reached after very short bidding sequences where South's shape is not shown. A side suit could be distributed thus:

$$K\ 7\ 4$$

$$\text{J led} \qquad\qquad A\ 8\ 5\ 3\ 2$$

$$?$$

After something like 1♣, Pass, 2♣, Pass, 4♣ what is East to do when dummy plays low without certain knowledge of the position of the queen?

This point will not be repeated again in detail but you will see that it applies to other systems discussed below and it will simply be referred to as 'the lower honour argument'.

iii) Continuing this argument, the nine could come from 9 x or 10 9 x making the count difficult to read.

ROMAN LEADS

This is a similar set-up to Blue Club leads with the king and ten classified as strong leads against no-trump contracts and other honours guarantee exactly one higher honour, the lower being led from touching honours. Similar arguments apply.

RUSINOW LEADS

Here again, the lower of touching honours is led, reversing with a doubleton.

An advantage is illustrated in this side suit against a trump contract:

                    10 7 5 4
    K Q   A 6 3 2
                    J 9 8

West leads the king followed by the queen and East can over-take, confident of a ruff on the third round. This may be important if he has no outside entry and three tricks in the suit are judged as necessary. On the other hand, if West leads the queen followed by the king, East will be confident that his partner can lead a third round. Playing standard leads, West leads the king in either case as the lead of the queen categorically denies the king and might be read as a singleton.

The lower honour argument applies against Rusinow leads.
Note that Rusinow leads apply only:
a) On trick one.
b) Against suit contracts.
c) If the suit led has not been bid by East.

BUSSO OR ATTITUDE LEADS

This applies to leads of spot cards and the principle here is that the lower the card you lead the more you like the suit and vice versa. Thus, for example, against a no-trump contract, you should lead:

a) the two from K J 8 7 5 2 because that is the suit on which you want to concentrate.
b) the nine from 9 5 2 to tell partner that you have no trick potential in the suit.
c) the six from Q 8 6 3 to suggest moderate interest.

The advantage here is that, above all other lead systems, it is best for the points roll-call.

The disadvantages are twofold:
i) It gives little indication of length although admittedly de-clarer is also deprived of that information.
ii) Very often, on the opening lead, it will not be clear whether

27

this is the right suit to attack. This particularly applies if you find East with a goodish holding in the suit. Furthermore, there is the problem of what to lead from such holdings as 10 9 8 7 2. You will probably want to concentrate on that suit against no-trumps but do you really want to lead the two? Also, how is East to read the 8 from K 10 9 8. The ten must be preferable but how will East read that?

JOURNALIST LEADS
This is a system combining Rusinow and Busso leads displaying a pleasing flexibility between no-trump and suit contracts.

Honour leads against no-trump contracts:

Ace: normally coming from a good suit, demands East to unblock an honour if he has it or give the count if he does not.

King: promises the queen or the ace but not both.

Queen: promises the jack, or may be from K Q 10 9 and in that case East is expected to unblock the jack if he has it.

Jack: denies a higher honour but promises the ten.

Ten: guarantees one of the top three and is led from holdings such as A 10 9, K 10 9, Q 10 9, A J 10, K J 10.

Nine: promises the ten but denies anything higher.

Spot cards are led according to the Busso system.

Against suit contracts, the Rusinow system applies to honour leads. For spot leads, the emphasis is on length.

If the number of cards held is:

 i) odd, lead the lowest card.

ii) even, lead the third highest.

A large number of recognised experts who use this system are convinced that it is the best and it is certainly a move towards the flexibility which is being advocated in this book. There is surely a clear-cut case for giving no-trump and suit contracts separate treatment rather than having one blanket rule for two markedly different scenarios. Nonetheless, the lower honour and other disadvantages indicated earlier still apply even ignoring the point that there is more to memorise which, for serious tournament players, should not be a prohibitive obstacle.

THE VINJE SYSTEM

This was set out in the book *New Ideas in Defensive Play* by the Norwegian expert of that name. It is not for me to reproduce the scores of pages of rules here but the main points will be summarised:

Aims:

1) To be adaptable between no-trump and suit contracts.
2) To ensure that the first card in a suit led gives as much information as possible.
3) To ensure the second card played by the hand who led the suit gives the count conclusively.
4) To give signals in a manner immune to deception from declarer.
5) To make due distinction between the opening lead and later stages of play.
6) To employ the two-card difference principle in as many situations as possible in the belief that partner ought, from the bidding, to be able to distinguish between suits of n cards or n − 2 or n + 2 and between honour holdings of none or two.

The rules for spot card leads are as follows:

Number of cards held	First card led	Second card led
2	1st	2nd
3	3rd	2nd
4	3rd	4th
5	5th	4th
6	4th	6th
7	7th	3rd

You see an obvious advantage here—with even holdings, you always play high, low and vice versa which certainly helps the individual suit roll-call.

The disadvantages appear to be threefold:

i) The lowest is led from x x x, which was discussed earlier.
ii) You have to lead the third card from four which can be expensive as here:

7 6 3

A Q 9 2   J 4

K 10 8 5

where, against a no-trump contract, the two clearly gains.

iii) The whole system is very distribution orientated and concentrates on the one suit rather than on the whole hand although Vinje allows use of discretion for suit-preference etc.

Vinje discards the rule of eleven for interpreting leads in favour of the rule of fourteen as follows.

Cards are numbered from 2 (deuce) to 14 (ace) and then:

Length of suit suggested by opening lead	Deduct number of card from
3	. 12
4	12
5	10
6	11
7	8

The Vinje distribution signals work well on this hand:

Hand No. 4
Dealer East
Game All

W	N	E	S
		Pass	2♣
Pass	2♢	Pass	2NT
Pass	3NT	end	

```
                      ♠ 10 7 5
                      ♡ 9 8 4
                      ♢ J 6 4
                      ♣ Q J 10 3
   ♠ A 9 2                             ♠ 8 6 3
   ♡ A J 7 5 2          N              ♡ 10 6 3
   ♢ 9 8 5          W       E          ♢ 10 3 2
   ♣ 7 4                S              ♣ K 6 5 2
                      ♠ K Q J 4
                      ♡ K Q
                      ♢ A K Q 7
                      ♣ A 9 8
```

After a straightforward Acol sequence in which South showed 23–24 balanced, West leads the two of hearts. When dummy plays low, East can see six cards and presumes his partner has five making eleven in all. He thus plays low. South wins and plays the king of spades and West, knowing the heart position, can win and confidently cash his hearts.

Playing standard leads, West would lead the five of hearts to the eight, ten and king and now, on the king of spades, West, in all honesty, would not have a clue what to do. He does not know whether the diamond jack is an entry or whether there is A K doubleton in clubs with South or a finesse position. It could easily be right to duck as South almost certainly has ♠ K Q J x and to win allows the ♠ 10 as an entry to dummy.

In order to discuss honour leads, we introduce a number of additions to bridge parlance. Honour sequences may be described as:

 i) Solid: three in a row like A K Q or K Q J.
 ii) Incomplete: break before lowest card as in A K J or K Q 10.
iii) Intermediate: break before second highest card as in A Q J or K Q 10.
iv) Partial: two touching honours as in A K x or Q J x.

When leading honours against no-trump contracts, we aim to:

a) Indicate the nature of the sequence unambiguously while giving partner the best chance to distinguish if any doubts should arise (and some are inevitable).
b) Enable partner to indicate the nature of his support accurately.

Leads follow the table below:

Card led	Nature of Sequence	Examples	Second honour led given an option
A	Partial	A K x	
K	Incomplete	A K J K Q 10	
Q	Solid or	A K Q x Q J 10 x	K (13) or A (14) to indicate odd or even number of cards held originally
	Partial	Q J x	
J	Solid or	K Q J x	K (13) or Q (12) to indicate odd or even number of cards held originally
	Intermediate or Jack high	A Q J x J 10 9 x J 10 8 x	
10	Intermediate, two higher honours or	A Q 10 9 x A J 10 x K J 10 x	
	Ten high	10 9 x	
9	Two higher non-touching honours or	A 10 9 x K 10 9 x Q 10 9 x	
	Nine high	9 8 x	

If you see the two-difference principle, it isn't quite as strenuous on the memory as it looks on a first reading. The ability to show count on the second lead is a useful extra but that could be incorporated into other systems. Even an agreement to lead king from A K Q could be supplemented by saying that the higher of the other two shows an even number and the lower an odd. Note again, original count is specified. In the later stages of play, this system sometimes stipulates that a player, notably East, shows current count.

Honour leads against suit contracts are orientated to finding out how many times a suit will stand up:

Card led	Holdings	Comments
A	A K x x	A (14) shows even number of cards. There is one exception in that the king is always led from A K (irrespective of leader's count) against a small slam and now East must give his count.
K	A K x	K (13) shows odd number of cards.
	K Q J x	Ambiguous: may be from A K x if A does not appear on dummy. Second lead shows length: Q (12) for even, J (11) for odd original holding.
	K Q	Consistent with the second lead of the queen showing an even number.
Q	A K Q x	Second lead shows length A (14) even, K (13) odd original holding.
	K Q x	Ambiguous: East does not know who will win first trick; the king is promised but if the ace is not with North, the points' and tricks' roll-calls are difficult.
J	Q J x	
10	A J 10 x K J 10 x J 10 x	Here the jack is always promised but there may be one or no honours with it and the two-difference principle doesn't operate.
9	A 10 9 x K 10 9 x Q 10 9 x 10 9 x	Here the ten is always promised and the jack always denied but again there may be one or no other honours.
8	K 9 8 x Q 9 8 x J 9 8 x 9 8 x	Nine promised, ten denied, same extra honour ambiguity.

From the right hand column, you can see the disadvantages at a glance even before the lower honour argument and short suit leads are taken into account. In addition, the insistence on varying the lead from A K according to your count in that suit rules out the facility to cash the 'wrong' card to indicate to partner that you intend to switch to a singleton. This is known as:

THE ALARM CLOCK LEAD

Another example of the type of lead designed to wake partner from his afternoon nap is that of a ridiculous card from an announced long suit in an attempt to pinpoint a devastating switch to partner—usually for a ruff as here:

West holds: ♠ K J 10 6 4 2
               ♡ 9 5 3
               ◇ —
               ♣ Q 8 7 5

and opens a weak 2♠. It is passed round to South who bids 4♡ and is allowed to play there. Now the lead of the ♠2 is anti-system unless you are playing attitude leads and alerts partner that there is something in the air; some authors describe this as an 'ODD BALL' and it can occur at later stages in the play as well as at trick one.

Despite all objections, those who play Vinje style are sure they are at the top of the market and to be fair, the content of the dummy hand and the bidding are bound to reduce the ambiguities considerably. Although there are hands where the Vinje method works better than its rivals, whether the extra effort pays dividends in the long term is possibly yet to be proved.

For the sake of completeness, there are a couple of other leads to be mentioned:

AMERICAN LEADS

These are now part of the Bridge 'Museum' being derived from whist to give partner a count when a long solid suit was being led.

As an example, the lead of a jack (from a suit headed by all the top honours) followed by the queen showed exactly seven; jack then king showed eight etc. Clearly Vinje has taken something from this idea.

TRELDE LEADS

This is a system of honour leads which attempts to distinguish between
1) A 'genuine' sequence: three touching honours and
2) A 'false' sequence: only two.
   The rules are as follows:

a) From suits headed by A K Q, interior sequences or A K doubleton, use your recognised practice.
b) From all other genuine sequences, K Q J, Q J 10, lead the highest card.
c) From false sequences lead the lower of the two honours.

The idea is that the contents of the North and East hands should clarify which sequence is being shown and the system looks a good variation on Rusinow noting, though, that the lower honour argument applies. There will also be problems if both North and East are very weak when the leads of K or Q may be ambiguous.

It might, therefore, be a good idea to adopt this system with the restriction that it will not apply if the bidding indicates that South is very strong and North very weak, typically if South has opened a strong club or Acol two bid and has received a negative reply.

CONCLUSION

Playing standard leads throughout my bridge career precludes me from giving a definite conclusion for lack of experience of the other methods. Perhaps however, when the extra information given to declarer, extra effort in learning and lower honour arguments are taken into account, the long-term advantage of

the various modern systems may, at best, be minimal. Nonetheless, these systems ought at least to be known and understood by
tournament players who will meet them as declarer with increas-
ing frequency.

The following is a possible recommendation:

Honour leads: Standard but K from A K doubleton against
suit contracts if you want a ruff and think it is
likely that partner can get in before trumps
are drawn. Q from A K Q and J from
A K Q J unless suit-preference considerations indicate otherwise.

Small trebletons: Do not make a hard and fast rule but tend
towards top of nothing against no-trump contracts and MUD against suits. Note the size of
your middle card and the message you feel is
most appropriate.

Longer suits of   Lead the top or second according to the size
small cards: of the top card and whether the top two cards
are touching, but note option to lead top card
if second card is deceptively small and attitude is considered of prime importance.

Three to an   Standard lowest card, but consider leading
honour: the honour of partner's bid suit if South is
known to be short and you are likely to want
to hold the lead for a switch through dummy
to partner's strong holding in another suit.

Longer suits   Standard fourth high, eight spot or lower, but
to one or   note the alarm clock option.
more honours:

Status of ten: Consider as honour if likely to help another
honour make a trick otherwise treat as low,
e.g. in top of nothing or MUD leads.

As a general rule, avoid underleading an ace against a suit
contract on trick one unless the bidding cries out for it. There are
basically three situations:

i) You consider it vital to get partner in at once, typically to
give you a ruff or lead to a tenace in another suit and this suit
represents the only chance of getting him in.

ii) Opponents have bid to five of a minor, having rejected 3NT because this suit is very weak and leading the ace may block the suit or allow a trick to the queen in South's hand:

```
                    9 6 4
     A Q 10 7 2                   K 5
                    J 8 3
```

or

```
                    8 7 3
        A 6 5 2                   K J 10
                    Q 9 4
```

iii) It is clear that North is very strong and South very weak and you believe that North may well have K J x in the suit and East Q x x or the like and you think that it is important that the suit be attacked immediately; otherwise play passive and let South do his own work—he may have difficulty in getting to his hand and may have to play the suit from the table.

If you agree on that, East has an easier time in this set-up:

```
                    7 5 4
     6 led                        K J 3 2
                    ?
```

With the ace marked in the South hand, East can smoke out the queen by playing the jack on trick one assisting his points roll-call.

3. Following to the Opening Lead

Big Brother is watching you!

We now move across the table to the East seat and look at the situation once the opening lead has been made and the dummy exposed. Good declarers will usually pause for a few seconds to make an overall plan and you should be using that time to make counter plans. Once a card is played from dummy, it is your turn.

If partner has led a low card and dummy has also played low, you will normally play as high as necessary in order to try and win this trick or to promote the defending side's cards, but note that there are exceptions as we shall see later.

Here, however, we shall primarily be concerned with situations in which partner and/or dummy play high cards and you will be following low. You can now give your partner a signal under one of the following basic headings:

1) Attitude—positive or negative—encouraging or discouraging regarding the suit led.
2) Distribution—odd or even number of cards in the suit led.
3) Suit preference—suggestion of a switch to a higher or lower ranking suit ignoring trumps or declarer's obvious long suit at no-trumps.
4) Other vital information.

We shall look at various systems of expressing these messages and their features. It is suggested that you proceed as follows:

a) Conduct your seven roll-calls, noting whether North's hand accurately reflects his bidding or whether he has clearly over/underbid.
b) Form some idea of what declarer's plan is likely to be.
c) Try to decide how many times you and/or your partner are likely to get in during the course of play. There is little point in suggesting a lead to partner if he has no chance of making it!
d) In the light of the information gathered so far, decide

whether you or your partner should be directing operations. If it is you, then you should try to make it clear that you have matters under control otherwise you should aim to give information to partner so that he can take command.

e) Consider following suit or (with a void) discarding, looking at 1), 2), 3), 4) in that order of priority, asking yourself what, if anything, partner needs to know and which of the four parameters, if more than one be relevant, is the most important. Remember, your partner should be thinking along the same lines.

'Oh, we ALWAYS give the count on trick one,' one pair proudly told me during a famous congress. '. . . and we are still waiting for our first bottom caused by playing that system!'

At the table, etiquette demanded that silence be observed. Let's give them the good news first: that bottom will never come. There are enough people around with a similar inflexible attitude to ensure that the worst they will get is a shared bottom. But now the bad news: there are all too many situations in which the count is of minimal or no relevance and that other messages must take precedence and therefore, while pairs who make 'simple and straightforward' rules like that will never strain themselves, they will equally never reach the top of the bridge ladder for lack of a consistently high standard of defence.

1) ATTITUDE:

There are three methods of expressing reaction towards the suit led:

a) **Standard**: a high card encourages and a low card discourages.
b) **Upside down**: a low card encourages and vice versa.

The majority of players prefer standard but the upside down signal has the edge in situations where East cannot spare a high card:

$$\begin{array}{ccc} & \text{Q 10 8 4} & \\ \text{A 7} & & \text{K J 9 2} \\ & \text{6 5 3} & \end{array}$$

On the lead of the ace, East will lose a trick if he follows with the nine; he must play the two and hope. Ideally, the two should be the encouraging card.

<pre>
                     8 3
    K Q 10 6   9 7 4
                     A J 5 2.
</pre>

On the lead of the king, the standard discouraging card is the four but now South may try a deceptive five and then West will wonder whether East has encouraged with A 4 2 or J 4 2. Playing upside down or 'reverse' signals, the nine is clearly discouraging.

However, the coin has two sides:

<pre>
                     A 7 4
    Q J 6   9 3 2
                     K 10 8 5
</pre>

On the lead of the queen against a trump contract followed by a low card from North, East is in trouble if he is playing upside down—if he plays a discouraging nine, he exposes his partner to a finesse while if he plays low, West is likely to expect the ten and lead the suit again when he next gets in. The standard discouraging card of the two keeps the defender's trick intact unless there is an endplay.

A case could be made for flexibility between the two and this is the idea behind a very recent development:

THE SCANIAN COMBINATION

This attempts to get the best of both worlds paying regard to two major factors applicable to the suit led:

 i) Has the dummy got a finessable card?
ii) How many cards do you, as East, hold?

For example, in this layout:

<pre>
                     K 6 5
    J 10 7 4   A 9 2
                     Q 8 3
</pre>

you need your high spot cards, here the nine for trick-taking purposes. When the jack is led, you want to encourage and here the reverse method is best. Similarly, where you have a long, strong suit:

$$\begin{array}{ccc} & \text{A J} & \\ \text{8 7 4} & & \text{K Q 10 2} \\ & \text{9 6 5 3} & \end{array}$$

you can ill-afford the high spot for encouragement when West leads to dummy's ace.

On the other hand, if you hold three cards or less, the reversed method can cost a trick either when discouraging from a weak short suit:

$$\begin{array}{ccc} & \text{9 4} & \\ \text{A K J 3} & & \text{10 8 2} \\ & \text{Q 7 6 5} & \end{array}$$

where the play of the eight on the ace will cost;
. . . or encouraging from a short strong suit:

$$\begin{array}{ccc} & \text{Q} & \\ \text{A K 8 6 3} & & \text{J 9 2} \\ & \text{10 7 5 4} & \end{array}$$

when it is necessary to throw the nine to unblock the run of the suit against no-trumps.

The suggested method is, therefore, the following:

If there is a finessable card on dummy, use the reversed method.

If not, use reversed if you hold four or more, normal with three or less.

The obvious question arises as to how West is supposed to know whether East is 'long' or 'short'. He cannot do so consistently and is thus deemed to be short unless:

 i) he has bid the suit.
 ii) when he has bid the suit first (in auctions where both partners bid it).
 iii) when he has made a lead-directing double of a cue-bid in the suit.

iv) when West's lead is known to be top of nothing or Q from
Q x etc.

The method of signalling used when the suit is led through
declarer later in the play is the converse:

If dummy has a finessable card, play normal otherwise play
reversed.

Here are three examples in each of which East leads the king:

```
                    J 8 4
      10 9 2                      K Q 6 5
                    A 7 3
```

West must play a discouraging two or lose a trick.

```
                    J 7 5 3
      A 9 2                       K Q 8 4
                    10 6
```

West must play the nine otherwise the suit will be blocked.

```
                    8 4
      A 9 2                       K Q 10 5
                    J 7 6 3
```

West plays the two to encourage, the nine is needed for trick-
taking.

The Swedish international who proposed this system looked at
countless suit combinations and it appears that he has an im-
provement on the exclusive use of either of the simple systems.
However, as will be explained in more detail when looking at the
Vinje system, there are objections, the principal one being that
we are looking at the suit in isolation rather than at the whole
hand. There is also the question of how a 'finessable' card is
defined.

c) **Odd and even**: here an odd card (9, 7, 5, 3) is encouraging
while an even card (10, 8, 6, 4, 2) is discouraging.
There are two advantages:
i) Absolute clarity. There is no argument as to which cards
are odd and which are even. With either of the other two

methods, there is scope for ambiguity—the 7 is low from 9 8 7 but high from K 7 3. The 4 is low from 9 8 4 but high from A 4 3 2.

ii) You can include a suit-preference option known as

THE WENCESLAUS SIGNAL

This covers situations where East, typically by an overcall or preemptive bid, is known to have a big suit—and now:

a) High odd card: encourages the suit.
b) High even: suit preference for higher ranking suit.
c) Low odd: suit preference for lower ranking suit.
d) Low even: discourages the suit.

The obvious disadvantage is that you may not hold the card you need for the signal—with 7 5 3, you can only encourage; with K 10 8 6, you can only discourage when, in each case, you want the opposite. Users of the system suggest that, to cover this situation, the lower the card, the more seriously it is taken. Thus the 3 is definitely encouraging but the 8 might be discouraging whereas the 2 is definitely discouraging.

2) DISTRIBUTION:

It is generally accepted that, where the count is considered relevant, a low card indicates an odd number while a high card shows an even number. Some experts recommend playing it the other way round, arguing that you are more likely to need your higher spot cards when you have an even number. Where you start with a high card, you follow with a lower card to complete a Peter or Echo.

A variant on the count used against no-trump contracts is:

THE FOSTER ECHO

The idea is to give partner the count, simultaneously unblocking where appropriate. The rule applies where East cannot beat the dummy:

 i) With two cards, play high then low.
 ii) With three, the second highest followed by the highest.
iii) With four, the second highest, then the third, then the fourth.

Examples in which West leads two top honours illustrate the advantages:

<pre>
                    9 4
    K Q J 6   8 7 3
                    A 10 5 2
</pre>

East plays 7 and 8 and unless South ducks again, the suit will run when East gets in. Unless East plays both his higher cards, South can win the second round and the suit will be blocked.

<pre>
                    7 3 2
    K Q J 9   8 6 5
                    A 10 4
</pre>

East plays 6 then 8 and if South wins the second round, West will know that the ten will fall on the third.

<pre>
                    2
    A K Q 10   9 7 6 5
                    J 8 4 3
</pre>

East plays 7 and 6 and West now knows that the jack will not fall. The major disadvantage of this echo is that, if East's first card is a low one, it may be very difficult to read.

3) SUIT PREFERENCE:

This is relatively rare on trick one and will be discussed in more detail later. Nevertheless, against a suit contract, there are at least three positions where it is relevant.

a) Where dummy has a singleton in the suit led and partner's lead is likely to hold the trick, you can play a high card to indicate values in the higher ranking suit and vice versa. Thus, if hearts are trumps and a winning spade honour is led, then a high spade would suggest a diamond, a low spade would point to clubs and a medium spade might be interpreted as:

   i) A wish to force dummy with a further spade.

  ii) No specific preference between the other two.

 iii) A suggestion that East's values are in spades and that West might switch to a trump.

It will usually be obvious which of the three applies.

b) Where West has led what is obviously a singleton and will want to know how to get East in to continue the suit.

c) Where West has led a suit which it is obviously ridiculous to continue, East will want to indicate a switch.

4) OTHER IMPORTANT INFORMATION:

Probably the most common situation is the playing of a solid honour card as here:

```
              8 6 5
   A K 2                     Q J 10 7 4
              9 3
```

On the lead of the ace, East can play the queen, denying the king but promising the jack. This would indicate that it is safe for West to underlead his king on trick two which may be important if the defenders consider that East, rather than West, should be on lead at trick three.

A similar position arises when, against a no-trump contract, West leads a suit in which East is void and has a long suit of his own. East may then indicate its nature by discarding a high honour, guaranteeing the one immediately below it and usually in practice, the next highest as well but not the one above. Thus East may discard Q from Q J 10 x x x and then if North has only small cards, West will know that it is safe to lead his king but that he must wait if he only has the ace. This can also apply against suit contracts where West leads a trump.

Having discussed the four possibilities, we now have to consider which one applies. As was mentioned earlier, situations are so varied that one cannot possibly make blanket rules. One reasonable guide, however, is that in situations where one defender is markedly stronger than the other, the strong hand should tend towards attitude to tell his partner what to play and the weak hand should tend towards distribution as his attitude is likely to be more or less known already.

Vinje, however, does make a list of rules dependent on what North turns up with, as the following examples illustrate:

At no-trumps, if partner leads a low card and dummy has low cards, the usual third hand high rule applies unless North and East hold spot cards only and the lead indicates:

i) a four- or five-card suit and it is clear that the number of cards held by West, North and East total eleven, or

ii) a six-card suit and North and East hold a total of five spot-cards between them, then East should play his lowest card. The theory will not be reproduced here in detail but if you work out the possibilities according to the lead system, you will see that, in these two circumstances, South must hold a doubleton honour which will come down and West will know the position.

Hand No. 4 in Chapter 1 should now be looked at again from East's point of view as a useful illustration.

Working out the various combinations and noting that there are certain situations where East's card is irrelevant, one can conclude that when North and East hold a total of five spot cards, East should play low if he can be confident that South holds at most a trebleton in the suit.

When following to an honour at no-trumps, East should give count in the normal way. When dummy holds honours, if East cannot win, he plays the same card that he would have led:

A Q

J 9 6 3   a) 10 8 7 2
                        b) 10 8 7 5 2

a) K 5 4
b) K 4

On the lead of the six to North's ace, East's 7 in a) will indicate a four-card suit and no hope while his 2 in b) will suggest three or five and West should be able from the bidding to work out which.

Vinje admits that declarer deception is possible in a number of situations and recommends the play of the second highest rather than third highest from four cards in certain holdings. This can lead to confusion between doubletons and four card suits but that also applies to standard petering.

When following to high honour sequence leads, the signal depends on what appears in dummy as follows:

i) If North has three or more cards, high honours should be unblocked unless it will obviously cost a trick to do so.
ii) Give count in the Vinje style if dummy holds three or more cards.
iii) Contribute missing sequence card if lead suggests incomplete sequence and both North and East hold exactly three cards.
iv) If dummy is short of the suit at no-trumps, give an attitude signal: positive if the complementing honour is held, negative followed by count otherwise, noting in this system, attitude signals are given on an upside-down basis.

There are further long lists of rules on how to follow on the basis that the honour lead is recognisable (and it isn't always). There is also a new signal for following honour leads against suit contracts called the trick-counting signal. East is expected to give this signal on the lead of the ace from ace, king and others if dummy has three or more small cards.

i) A low card expresses the belief that the defenders can take one or three tricks in the suit by virtue of one of the following:
   a) Cashing on top.
   b) East ruffing the third round.
   c) East leading J 10 through South's queen.
ii) The third lowest card indicates two defensive tricks in the suit.

Trick count may also be given if North holds x x or Q x. Where he holds a singleton, suit preference is recommended.

We could discuss possibilities for hours but the principal objections seem to be:

a) The amount that has to be memorised.
b) The concentration on the details of the suit led which may not always be of prime importance when considering the hand as a whole.
c) The whole system is based on East giving information to West and while this will be sensible most of the time particularly if West's first card is likely to be a winner, it may not always be appropriate.
d) Most of the defences which the system claims to find can be worked out by roll-calling and use of discretion.

We shall now look at four simple examples. Assume you have agreed to play the modified form of standard leads recommended in Chapter 1:

Hand No. 5
Dealer East
E–W Vulnerable

W	N	E	S
		Pass	1♡
Dble	2NT	Pass	4♡
end			

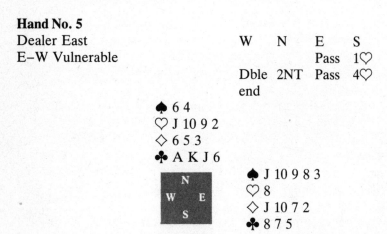

♠ 6 4
♡ J 10 9 2
♢ 6 5 3
♣ A K J 6

♠ J 10 9 8 3
♡ 8
♢ J 10 7 2
♣ 8 7 5

North's 2NT showed a good raise to 3♡. West leads the queen of spades and dummy plays the four; plan your defence.

Hand No. 6

Dealer South
N–S Vulnerable

W	N	E	S
			1♡
Pass	3♡	Pass	3♠
Pass	4◇	Pass	6♡
end			

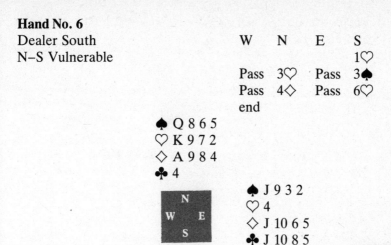

♠ Q 8 6 5
♡ K 9 7 2
◇ A 9 8 4
♣ 4

♠ J 9 3 2
♡ 4
◇ J 10 6 5
♣ J 10 8 5

North–South have agreed to play Blue Club style cue bids and so the 3♠ and 4◇ bids guaranteed first or second round controls in those suits. Partner leads the ace of spades to dummy's five; plan your defence.

Hand No. 7

Dealer North
Love All

W	N	E	S
	Pass	Pass	1♠
Pass	2♠	Pass	4♠
end			

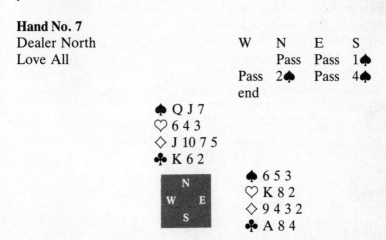

♠ Q J 7
♡ 6 4 3
◇ J 10 7 5
♣ K 6 2

♠ 6 5 3
♡ K 8 2
◇ 9 4 3 2
♣ A 8 4

North–South are playing Acol with five-card majors. Partner leads the queen of hearts to dummy's three; plan your defence.

Hand No. 8
Dealer East
E–W Vulnerable

W	N	E	S
		2♠	4♡
		end	

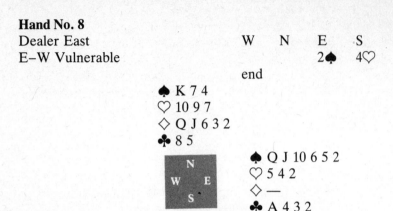

♠ K 7 4
♡ 10 9 7
♢ Q J 6 3 2
♣ 8 5

♠ Q J 10 6 5 2
♡ 5 4 2
♢ —
♣ A 4 3 2

Your opener showed 6–9 points and exactly six spades. Partner leads the ace of spades to dummy's four; plan your defence.

Solutions:

Hand No. 5
West's double almost certainly promises a spade suit and the queen clearly comes from A K Q or, more hopefully A K Q x. The defence will obviously have to attack diamonds but the suit will probably best be led from your hand. The only way you can get in is for partner to underlead his spades at trick two. To make this clear, you should play your jack under the queen to promise the ten.

The deal:

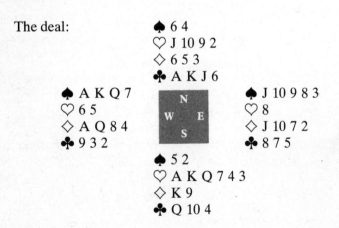

♠ 6 4
♡ J 10 9 2
♢ 6 5 3
♣ A K J 6

♠ A K Q 7
♡ 6 5
♢ A Q 8 4
♣ 9 3 2

♠ J 10 9 8 3
♡ 8
♢ J 10 7 2
♣ 8 7 5

♠ 5 2
♡ A K Q 7 4 3
♢ K 9
♣ Q 10 4

50

Now the defence can take their two diamonds to defeat the game. Note the advantage of leading the queen from A K Q rather than ace or king. Possibly, the jack might still work but if West is missing the queen, he might simply take it that East is making a suit preference signal for diamonds which would be important if he held the king. If any event, the situation is a lot less clear.

Hand No. 6
This trick may well be ruffed or South may have the king of spades singleton. In either case, it probably will not matter very much which card you play. It will be more important if South has a small singleton and you should confirm the count by playing the nine, encouragement/discouragement of the suit led and suit preference being of minimal importance here. In particular, you will ensure that South does not get away with daylight robbery.

The deal:

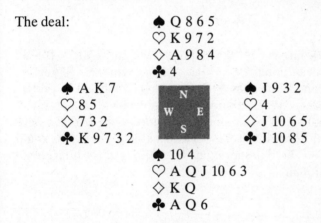

```
                  ♠ Q 8 6 5
                  ♡ K 9 7 2
                  ♢ A 9 8 4
                  ♣ 4
   ♠ A K 7                        ♠ J 9 3 2
   ♡ 8 5           N              ♡ 4
   ♢ 7 3 2      W     E           ♢ J 10 6 5
   ♣ K 9 7 3 2     S              ♣ J 10 8 5
                  ♠ 10 4
                  ♡ A Q J 10 6 3
                  ♢ K Q
                  ♣ A Q 6
```

This hand represents our first visit to the tangled world of deception. More and more it will be found that, in top-class tournaments, players are making these lead-inhibiting bids. Only clear and relevant signalling and interpretation will bring them to justice. We shall discuss deception in play and defence in more detail later.

Hand No. 7
Here you will want hearts to be continued and should say so by playing the eight. Unless this line is followed, South can set up diamond tricks for discards using the high trumps as entry to dummy.

The deal:

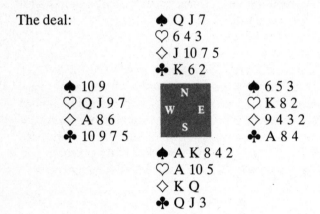

```
                    ♠ Q J 7
                    ♡ 6 4 3
                    ◇ J 10 7 5
                    ♣ K 6 2
   ♠ 10 9                          ♠ 6 5 3
   ♡ Q J 9 7          N            ♡ K 8 2
   ◇ A 8 6        W       E        ◇ 9 4 3 2
   ♣ 10 9 7 5         S            ♣ A 8 4
                    ♠ A K 8 4 2
                    ♡ A 10 5
                    ◇ K Q
                    ♣ Q J 3
```

Note the advantage over the 'count every time' addicts. If East plays a distributional two, West might well read South for ♡ A K 10 and if East has ♣ A Q, a club switch will be preferable to a heart continuation when he gets in with the diamond ace on trick two. West cannot really afford to duck to get more information from you because South's king of diamonds could be a singleton. Your desperation ◇ 9 might again be interpreted as distributional.

Hand No. 8

You might have been tempted to double 4♡ to request an unusual lead but as N–S may be close to a slam, you may have decided that a redouble could result in a considerable loss. At this stage, you do not know how many spades your partner holds but what is clear is that you must shout for a diamond switch. This means an unnecessarily high card and your best shot is the jack. The queen might be interpreted as top of a long solid sequence indicating that it is safe for partner to continue the suit.

The deal:

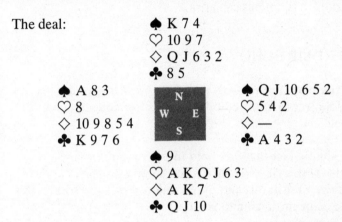

```
                    ♠ K 7 4
                    ♡ 10 9 7
                    ◇ Q J 6 3 2
                    ♣ 8 5
    ♠ A 8 3                        ♠ Q J 10 6 5 2
    ♡ 8             N              ♡ 5 4 2
    ◇ 10 9 8 5 4  W   E            ◇ —
    ♣ K 9 7 6       S              ♣ A 4 3 2
                    ♠ 9
                    ♡ A K Q J 6 3
                    ◇ A K 7
                    ♣ Q J 10
```

The defence will continue on suit-preference lines: if West's ace of spades is a singleton, he will lead a high diamond but here, where his re-entry is in clubs, the four is the correct card to defeat the game by two tricks. Note that, with strong holdings in the other three suits, South must lead a trump to inflict a similar result on 4♠ by East.

Notice that these four hands illustrated the four basic types of signal available. In the following chapters, we shall see how the defender uses his discretion to decide which of them is relevant at later stages in the play as well as on trick one. Although we shall be giving the various types new and amusing names to assist with memory, we shall see that all of them belong to one of these four categories.

4. *The Distributional Kaleidoscope*

So teach us, Oh Lord, to number our days,
And clubs and diamonds and hearts and spades!

In this chapter, we shall be looking in more detail at a number of situations in which distributional signals apply and illustrate areas in which problems can arise.

THE TRUMP ECHO

This is the play, normally from a three-card trump holding, of the middle trump followed by the lowest to indicate one of the following:

1) The simple fact that you hold three (on rare occasions five) trumps with a view to help partner count the hand as a whole.
2) A desire to ruff; this may apply with two or more trumps but three is the most common case.
3) Suit preference.
4) The Vinje distributional split.
5) Other vital information.

To be realistic, the vast majority of partnerships play 1) and/or 2) and leave it at that. Those who have agreed to play Vinje signals throughout are likely to stick to 4) almost exclusively. It is possible, however, that use of discretion can allow a good partnership, who do not play Vinje signals, to use all the other four as and when they apply. It should be noted that, with three low trumps, there are no less than six different ways in which you can follow as trumps are being drawn and therefore, it is usually possible to send more than one message. Again, the important thing to consider is what partner, if anything, needs to know.

Before considering the trump peter, you should ask yourself a number of questions:

a) Is it clear that all the trumps are going to be drawn? If so, indicating a ruff is irrelevant as is your count in trumps as you will play them all, anyway, for partner to see.

b) If trumps are not all going to be drawn and you are going to be left with at least one, do you want to ruff, i.e. is that remaining trump going to be a master and even if it isn't, might not a ruff be more helpful to declarer, allowing one of dummy's low trumps to become an entry to a long suit which would be dead otherwise?

c) If your remaining trump is low, will it be obvious to partner that there is no suit that you could possibly ruff and in that case, is there a message you wish to send under 3) or 5) above?

d) If a ruff is on, are you sure you will not merely be ruffing a loser or are you sitting over a winning card on dummy in which case there will be an obvious gain?

As you see, it is again down to the seven roll-calls and it may well be best to start with some examples. Try and decide what information is relevant.

Hand No. 9
Dealer East
E–W Vulnerable

W	N	E	S
		1◇	1♡
Pass	4♡	end	

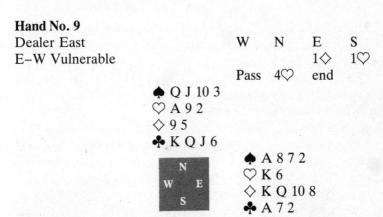

♠ Q J 10 3
♡ A 9 2
◇ 9 5
♣ K Q J 6

♠ A 8 7 2
♡ K 6
◇ K Q 10 8
♣ A 7 2

Partner leads the nine of spades and dummy plays the three. The lead is unlikely to be a singleton as South, holding both majors, would probably have doubled rather than overcalled. That, however, is a small point. You have an outside entry so you win, South playing the four. You return the two of spades to indicate the ace of clubs if partner does ruff. (This will be discussed in more detail under 'suit-preference' later.)

Actually, South wins with the king, partner playing the six. Obviously, South fears a ruff and so rejects the trump finesse and plays a low heart towards the ace and returns the two as partner follows with the seven and three. Winning with the king of trumps, how do you continue?

Hand No. 10

Dealer South

Game All

W	N	E	S
			1♠
Pass	3NT	Pass	6♠
end			

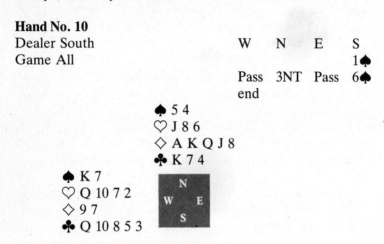

```
              ♠ 5 4
              ♡ J 8 6
              ◇ A K Q J 8
              ♣ K 7 4
  ♠ K 7              N
  ♡ Q 10 7 2     W       E
  ◇ 9 7              S
  ♣ Q 10 8 5 3
```

A number of comments could be made about the bidding of this hand but particularly with long solid suits around, it is very often good to 'bash' the final contract rather than give the opponents a long lecture on how to plan their defence. Modern day 'lengthy conversation' buffs would, no doubt, disagree. Anyway, we are not here to discuss opponents' bidding; we have enough problems of our own!

The first question is: 'What do you lead?' Bidding like this usually calls for busy defence before those long suits come in but North's 3NT bid is likely to show a balanced hand and you know that your king of spades is almost certain to be well-placed. You therefore decide to go for the relatively passive nine of diamonds and regret it when you see dummy. The ace wins, East playing the five and South the two, and South then plays the five of spades to partner's ten and his queen. Quick! How do you defend?

Hand No. 11

Dealer East
N–S Vulnerable

W	N	E	S
		Pass	1♡
Pass	3NT	Pass	4♣
Pass	4♢	Pass	4♠
Pass	6♡	end	

♠ J 9
♡ K 10 8 2
♢ A K 9
♣ K 10 7 3

♠ Q 10 7 5 3
♡ 9
♢ J 8 7 2
♣ J 5 2

This was a Precision sequence in which South originally promised 11–15 with at least five hearts and North's 3NT showed 14–15 with four trumps and a balanced hand, i.e. a good raise to game. Cue-bidding followed. Prospects do not look good and you decide that the best chance is to find partner with help in spades. You therefore lead the five of spades to the nine, king and ace. South now draws two rounds of trumps, partner following with the six and three and plays three rounds of diamonds, ruffing the third in hand. Now comes the eight of spades which you win as partner follows with the two. How do you continue?

r's peter in trumps clearly indicates a third trump and his
…h spades has shown a doubleton. A spade ruff is, therefore,
…able and you should play one. Had West not petered in
trumps, you would have had to attack diamonds immediately,
hoping to take a trick in each suit off your own bat.

The deal:

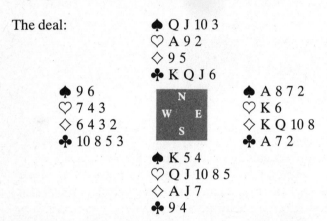

```
                        ♠ Q J 10 3
                        ♡ A 9 2
                        ◇ 9 5
                        ♣ K Q J 6
    ♠ 9 6                                ♠ A 8 7 2
    ♡ 7 4 3              N               ♡ K 6
    ◇ 6 4 3 2         W     E            ◇ K Q 10 8
    ♣ 10 8 5 3           S               ♣ A 7 2
                        ♠ K 5 4
                        ♡ Q J 10 8 5
                        ◇ A J 7
                        ♣ 9 4
```

Continuing spades in the latter case would cost an important
tempo and allow South to knock out the ace of clubs and discard
both his diamond losers: one on the long spade, the other on a
club honour.

Hand No. 10

On this bidding, it is not out of the question that South has eight
spades in which case partner's trump is a singleton and meaning-
less. However, if South has only seven spades, partner's card is a
peter and you must decide what for. It is unlikely on the bidding
that South has only six spades and because he failed to open two
spades, he may well be short on high card points. It is a far better
bet that partner has an ace rather than a desire to ruff. Had he a
void in clubs or hearts, he surely would have doubled for a lead.
If you have hit a singleton diamond, that would leave South with
five low cards in the suit in which case he would be something like
7 1 5 0 if his bidding makes any sense. That singleton, in clubs or
hearts, would have to be the ace in which case he could ensure his

58

contract by playing out ace and another spade, happy to lose one trick to the king. No, the best chance is to read partner's ten as suit preference, switch to a heart and hope.

The deal:

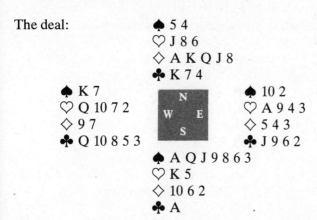

```
              ♠ 5 4
              ♡ J 8 6
              ◇ A K Q J 8
              ♣ K 7 4
♠ K 7                          ♠ 10 2
♡ Q 10 7 2                     ♡ A 9 4 3
◇ 9 7                          ◇ 5 4 3
♣ Q 10 8 5 3                   ♣ J 9 6 2
              ♠ A Q J 9 8 6 3
              ♡ K 5
              ◇ 10 6 2
              ♣ A
```

Perhaps you were put off by that 'Quick!'. This is not one of those situations where you have to duck in your sleep, hoping that declarer will cross to dummy and repeat the finesse, wasting a valuable entry in the process. But you have to be on the look out for such positions. You noticed that East did his best at trick one, attitude and distribution in diamonds being irrelevant.

Hand No. 11

Partner's trump peter was intended to stop declarer giving you the wrong impression. Assuming that trumps have been drawn completely, South appears to have started with a 2 6 2 3 shape and you will have to open up the clubs or give a fatal ruff and discard. In that event, your best play is probably the jack of clubs and South will now get home if he plays for the (most likely) position of divided honours. Partner has, however, told you that he has a third trump. This leaves South with four clubs and giving a ruff and discard is perfectly safe if East has the queen of clubs as indeed he must to give you any chance at all. You should, therefore, play another spade or a diamond.

The deal:

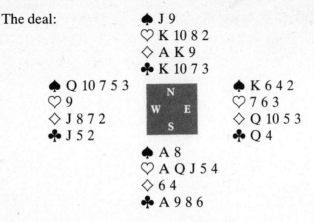

	♠ J 9	
	♡ K 10 8 2	
	◇ A K 9	
	♣ K 10 7 3	
♠ Q 10 7 5 3		♠ K 6 4 2
♡ 9		♡ 7 6 3
◇ J 8 7 2		◇ Q 10 5 3
♣ J 5 2		♣ Q 4
	♠ A 8	
	♡ A Q J 5 4	
	◇ 6 4	
	♣ A 9 8 6	

Did you attach any significance to the two of spades by East on the second round? We shall discuss this later in the chapter.

VINJE SPLIT

We have thus seen examples covering the first three possible messages. The Vinje approach encourages petering with two or more trumps in order to give a guide to the whole distribution. There are in all 39 hand patterns ranging from the most balanced 4 3 3 3 to the extreme 13 0 0 0. These can be divided into two distinct categories:

a) Those in which three suits have an odd number of cards and the remaining suit has an even number, e.g. 4 3 3 3, 5 3 3 2, 8 3 1 1 which will be called a unique even hand.

b) Those in which three have an even number and the remaining suit has an odd number, e.g. 4 4 3 2, 5 4 2 2, 7 4 2 0, a unique odd hand.

Although 16 out of the 39 fall into category a) against 23 into b) the probability of picking up one type or the other is almost exactly 50–50, primarily because most of the rare freaks fall into category b). This is an excellent illustration of the Vinje signal in action:

Hand No. 12

Dealer West
E–W Vulnerable

W	N	E	S
Pass	Pass	Pass	2NT
Pass	3♣	Pass	3♢
Pass	4♢	Pass	4♡
Pass	5♣	Pass	6♢
end			

```
                        ♠ J 9
                        ♡ J 6
                        ♢ K 10 8 4 2
                        ♣ A 10 8 4
     ♠ K 8 7 6           N
     ♡ K 10 8 7 3      W   E
     ♢ 5                  S
     ♣ Q J 7
```

South's opening bid promised 22–23 balanced and three clubs was Baron. Once the diamond fit had been found cue-bidding led to the slam.

You have a difficult hand to lead from and a trump seems best. Dummy plays low and your partner's six loses to South's ace. Declarer now plays a second round of trumps, East following with the nine and then plays three rounds of clubs. You win the third, all following. What do you lead now and would it make any difference if partner had played the nine and six of trumps in that order rather than the other way round?

Vinje argues that, thanks to the trump peter, you should know what to do. By playing his trumps low–high, East has shown you three even suits and one odd suit. On the assumption that South has drawn all the trumps, East must be 4 4 2 3, remembering that South must be reasonably balanced to have opened 2NT. Thus, on a points roll-call, East must have zero and South is now waiting for you with ♠ A Q x and ♡ A Q doubleton.

You must, therefore, exit with a heart and wait for your spade trick. Were you to exit with a spade, South could discard his queen of hearts on the long club and cross-ruff the rest for his slam.

Had East played his trumps the other way round, however, you would now know that he started with 5 3 2 3 and that South was now holding ♠ A Q doubleton and ♡ A Q x and now you must exit with a spade and wait for a heart trick.

The deal:

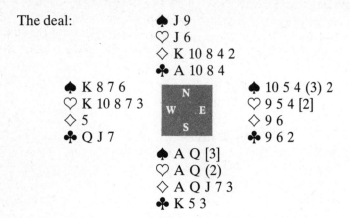

```
                        ♠ J 9
                        ♡ J 6
                        ◇ K 10 8 4 2
                        ♣ A 10 8 4
    ♠ K 8 7 6                              ♠ 10 5 4 (3) 2
    ♡ K 10 8 7 3          N               ♡ 9 5 4 [2]
    ◇ 5              W         E           ◇ 9 6
    ♣ Q J 7              S                 ♣ 9 6 2
                        ♠ A Q [3]
                        ♡ A Q (2)
                        ◇ A Q J 7 3
                        ♣ K 5 3
```

Full credit to the ingenuity but let us see if we could have found the correct defence without using that trump peter.

Even assuming that two rounds of trumps cleared East's holding and with that method this certainly is not proved, how does West know East's lengths in the majors? First of all, South's hand, as far as points are concerned, is announced almost exactly. West knows that East has no points and East is likely to know that his partner realises this; therefore, count if anything, is the message to send. What should be considered is the manner in which East follows to those three rounds of clubs. To be strict, as East has three clubs, he should see to it that his second card is higher than his first but even now, there are three ways of following to the suit. Let's try the following:

a) 2 6 9: odd number of clubs, emphasis on hearts.
b) 2 9 6: odd number of clubs, emphasis on spades.
c) 6 9 2: odd number of clubs, equal length in the majors.

All very intricate but with a slam at stake, is it not worth it?

In fairness, the trump peter has its merits but it should probably be considered a very delicate tool. A number of problems could arise:

i) In the type of situation given above, East could peter or fail to peter in trumps at will but suppose another hand comes up where dummy is very weak and playing low on trick one might permit declarer a valuable entry there? Does playing third hand high constitute a trump peter?

ii) As explained before, this trump peter does not clarify the trump length and there may be ambiguity if South does not draw all the trumps.

iii) The suit-preference option is lost; that could be important as there are many situations in which count is irrelevant.

Nonetheless, it is good to see a move in the direction sought in this book—the ability to give the count in one suit by petering in another. However, perhaps it can be done more accurately with a signal which might be called:

THE LONE RANGER

This is primarily orientated towards the consideration of an isolated long suit in dummy. It may be necessary for a defender, notably West, to know the count before the suit is touched.

This was the hand that inspired the new signal. Take the East seat and see if you can defeat your author as South:

Hand No. 13
Dealer South
E–W Vulnerable

W	N	E	S
			1◇
Pass	2♣	Pass	2NT
Pass	3NT	end	

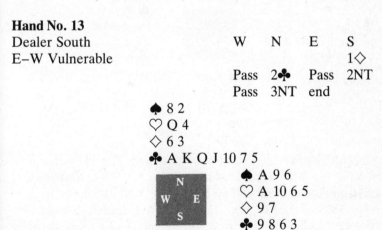

♠ 8 2
♡ Q 4
◇ 6 3
♣ A K Q J 10 7 5

            ♠ A 9 6
            ♡ A 10 6 5
            ◇ 9 7
            ♣ 9 8 6 3

This was a Precision sequence and South's opening bid showed 11–15 with three or more diamonds. North's 2♣ showed a suit and asked for strength and major suit stoppers. This is played strictly and South's 2NT promised a stop in both majors and 11–13. He may or may not be void of clubs.

Partner leads a fourth-high five of spades to the two, your ace and South's four. You return the nine to the jack, queen and eight. Partner persists with the three, showing that he started with a five-card suit, declarer winning with the king as dummy throws a diamond. South now goes into a long trance and has clearly got problems. Eventually, he plays the king of hearts. West plays the two and dummy the four; plan your defence.

This is a beautiful example of the use of the 'What, if anything, does partner need to know?' question. If South is void of clubs, you will have to duck this trick. If not, you will have to win and play West for the diamond ace. Either way, you are going to look very silly if you get it wrong. When the hand came up in a practice session, East, a life master, decided that declarer's problem was obviously a club void and ducked without giving the matter a second thought.

The deal:

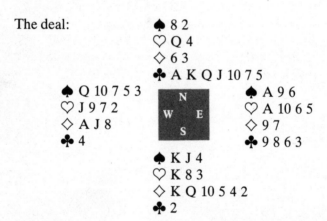

```
                  ♠ 8 2
                  ♡ Q 4
                  ◇ 6 3
                  ♣ A K Q J 10 7 5
♠ Q 10 7 5 3                          ♠ A 9 6
♡ J 9 7 2          N                  ♡ A 10 6 5
◇ A J 8        W   E                   ◇ 9 7
♣ 4                S                   ♣ 9 8 6 3
                  ♠ K J 4
                  ♡ K 8 3
                  ◇ K Q 10 5 4 2
                  ♣ 2
```

You can now see what South's problem was. The first step was to roll-call the red aces. If East has both, there was no difficulty; if he had neither, there was no chance. If West had the heart ace, again there was no chance. The critical case lay in the possibility of West holding the diamond and East the heart. To play down the clubs would allow endless signalling. If South was going to go in for stealing, it would have to be done immediately. The best chance seemed to be to try and give the impression of a void of clubs and an attempt to set up the queen of hearts as entry. East duly got the message and gave away the ninth trick.

But now let us look at the defence in more detail. When the problem was presented, did you attach any significance to that two of hearts? Before going further, perhaps we can look at the problem again but this time from West's point of view. Remember that we had the three rounds of spades, the long trance from South and the king of hearts. Which card would you have played? Did you agree with that two?

Roll-calling, you can see your partner's problem. He clearly has the ace of hearts and will be wondering whether to take it. The vital information is the distribution of clubs! By playing the two of hearts, you showed an odd number (of clubs: the count of hearts is irrelevant). East now knows that the outstanding clubs are 1–1 and must therefore take the heart ace and switch to diamonds. Had you shown an even number, East would have had to decide whether this was a doubleton or a void so I have only taken a step towards solving the problem which works perfectly on this deal but not necessarily every time.

Note that Vinje signals are not good enough here. Even if it was agreed that West's card to the heart trick is a Vinje split signal, a high card showing three 'odd' suits and one even could come from 5 4 3 1 or from 5 3 3 2 and East is none the wiser. A low card could come from 5 4 2 2 or 5 4 4 0 and the ambiguity is still there.

Perhaps we can set down a guide for situations when this signal applies:

a) When there is an isolated long suit on dummy.
b) In a suit contract where dummy has something like K J x x x and South is likely to lead what may well be a singleton through partner's ace.

Thus you will see that this is a signal usually given by East to West although the 'original' showed an example of the contrary.

Albert Benjamin clearly foresaw the idea when he introduced:

THE BENJAMIN TRUMP SIGNAL
This covers situations in which a defender, holding trumps of equal value, for example 9 8, could play them in a specific order

to indicate his count in another suit. Benjamin named this the 'count suit'. In the context of the trump suit itself, the order in which you play does not matter so if you peter, that shows an even number of cards in the count suit and vice versa.

Benjamin suggested that, in principle, the count suit should be the highest ranking suit as yet untouched. This does give clarity but that specific suit may be of no interest to the proceedings and as you have to follow in trumps one way or the other, you may run the risk of helping declarer and/or deceiving partner.

Still on the subject of long suits in dummy (or in declarer's hand), another method of giving count is:

THE REO RULE OF EVEN AND ODD

When following to an enemy suit, an even numbered card shows an even number of cards in the suit and vice versa. Where a defender does not hold a card of the necessary parity, he peters.

The advantages and disadvantages were explained in Chapter 2. Notably here, it may take two rounds for absolute clarity which could well be too late in trick-stealing situations.

It was mentioned before that, when one defender is very weak, his prime aim is to give his partner the count in various suits. We are now going to look at two more distributional signals with this principle in mind:

THE BECHGAARD ECHO

This is used to give lengths of long weak suits as follows:

Length	Order	Example
3	up the line	3 5 7
4	one peter	5 3 7 8
5	delayed peter	5 6 3 7 8
6	repeated peter	5 3 2 6 7 8
7	double peter	4 2 6 5 7 8 9

Try this as an example:

Hand No. 14
Dealer South
E–W Vulnerable

W	N	E	S
			2♣
Pass	2♦	Pass	6♡
Pass	7♡	end	

♠ J 7
♡ K
♦ J 10 8 6 5 4 3 2
♣ J 4

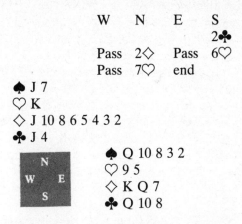

♠ Q 10 8 3 2
♡ 9 5
♦ K Q 7
♣ Q 10 8

South has the sort of hand which, as far as you're concerned, must remain in the realms of Dreamland. Note the sequence is invitational to a grand slam whereas a direct opening bid of 6♡ is much more preemptive and should be passed by North with the above holding.

Partner observes a well-known principle that you should usually lead a trump against a grand slam. South overtakes and continues with trumps, West following twice more and then discarding the five and three of clubs. You can afford two low spades and the seven of diamonds. On the sixth heart, partner discards the two of clubs. Dummy has discarded diamonds throughout; plan your defence. Would it make any difference if West had played his clubs in the order 3 5 2?

Here, the Bechgaard echo will save you from an unpleasant guess. In the first case, West has shown you six clubs and you can discard all yours with impunity, secure in the knowledge that your holding is useless. You will then wait for a count on the spades, which partner must give on the last trump and you will know whether to keep that suit or diamonds when South cashes his top clubs.

Where partner shows you only five clubs, you must keep your holding intact, confident that your queen will score:

The deal:

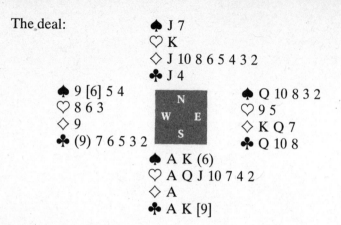

```
                        ♠ J 7
                        ♡ K
                        ◇ J 10 8 6 5 4 3 2
                        ♣ J 4
    ♠ 9 [6] 5 4                              ♠ Q 10 8 3 2
    ♡ 8 6 3            N                     ♡ 9 5
    ◇ 9             W      E                 ◇ K Q 7
    ♣ (9) 7 6 5 3 2     S                    ♣ Q 10 8
                        ♠ A K (6)
                        ♡ A Q J 10 7 4 2
                        ◇ A
                        ♣ A K [9]
```

The other signal designed to help partner to count a long suit is:

THE SIX-SHOOTER

This is the discard of an unnecessarily high card from a suit of exactly six. As well as helping partner with discards, it can pinpoint a void in declarer's hand and the consequence that a strong holding in dummy cannot be reached, a similar situation to the Lone Ranger original. Note that this idea can be extended to longer suits as follows:

Seven: Discard lowest card (odd number) then the six-shooter.

Eight: Discard second lowest, then the lowest (petering with even number) then the six-shooter.

Nine: Discard three lowest cards up the line (odd) then the six-shooter, and so on.

Try an example:

Hand No. 15
Dealer East
E–W Vulnerable

W	N	E	S
		1NT	4♠
	end		

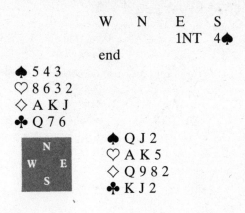

♠ 5 4 3
♡ 8 6 3 2
♢ A K J
♣ Q 7 6

♠ Q J 2
♡ A K 5
♢ Q 9 8 2
♣ K J 2

Your opener showed 15–17.

Partner leads the seven of hearts and you play three rounds. All follow, South having started with Q J 10. He now plays the ace of trumps. How do you plan your defence if partner discards:

a) the ten of diamonds,

b) the four of diamonds?

Solution:

Hand No. 15

The bidding marks West with little or nothing and that ten is clearly trying to tell you something. If you read it as a six-shooter, you can roll-call the suit and give South a void. That means that, on the third round of trumps you will be end-played, forced to lead round to dummy in one of the minors. But now roll-call the trump suit and declarer's tricks and you will realise that by throwing your honours under South's, you can hold him to the nine tricks in his own hand.

69

The deal:

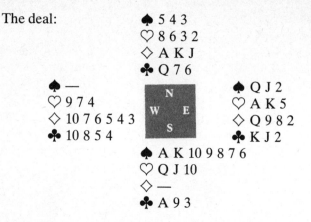

♠ 5 4 3
♥ 8 6 3 2
♢ A K J
♣ Q 7 6

♠ —
♥ 9 7 4
♢ 10 7 6 5 4 3
♣ 10 8 5 4

♠ Q J 2
♥ A K 5
♢ Q 9 8 2
♣ K J 2

♠ A K 10 9 8 7 6
♥ Q J 10
♢ —
♣ A 9 3

If West fails to indicate the six-card diamond suit, you will have to hold your trump honours and play partner for the ace of clubs leaving South with six trump tricks, two diamonds and the queen of hearts.

There is nothing to prevent a partnership from using both the Bechgaard echo and the six-shooter. The advantages and disadvantages are as follows:

i) The Bechgaard echo deals with all lengths while the six-shooter can only cope with six-card or longer suits.
ii) The six-shooter gives the message immediately while the Bechgaard echo takes three rounds.
iii) Nevertheless, you may have to use the Bechgaard echo for six-card or longer suit in situations where you cannot afford the high card, as in K 6 5 4 3 2.

So far we have looked at situations in which count has been suggested on the first round of the suit and perhaps confirmed if a second round has been played. We are now going to consider the possibility of giving count on the second round of a suit during hands in which a player is obliged to lead or follow with an honour on the first. In these cases, of course, the partner has little or no indication of length.

THE AMMETER

The term is borrowed from the sphere of electricity. The ammeter is a machine which measures current or, more literally, counts amps. Here, we are trying to give current count after having played an honour first time. We use the normal method, low for odd number (originally even) and vice versa. (There is nothing to stop you petering according to your original count but be sure to agree it with your partner.) There are a number of situations in which the ammeter is useful, most notably to tell you how often a suit will stand up in a trump contract. Try a couple of examples, remembering that the information given should be used to roll-call the whole hand.

Hand No. 16

Dealer South

E–W Vulnerable

W	N	E	S
			1♡
Pass	2♡	Pass	4♡
end			

♠ 8 5 3
♡ J 7 5
◇ A 8 6 5 2
♣ 7 6

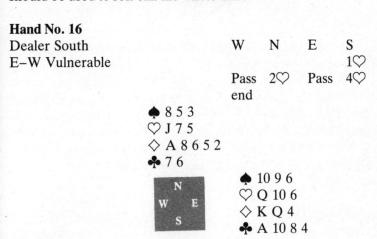

♠ 10 9 6
♡ Q 10 6
◇ K Q 4
♣ A 10 8 4

Partner leads the queen of clubs to the six, ace and five. You observe that this contract is unlikely to make unless that diamond suit can be brought in and therefore set about attacking dummy's entries by persisting with clubs and return the four. South's king wins as West follows with the three and South plays the seven of diamonds to the nine and dummy's two; plan your defence.

Would it make any difference if partner's second club had been the nine?

Hand No. 17
Dealer East
N–S Vulnerable

W	N	E	S
		Pass	1NT
Pass	2NT	Pass	3NT
end			

♠ A Q J
♡ 5
♢ K 7 6 5 4
♣ Q 9 7 3

♠ 7 3 2
♡ A K 9 4 2
♢ Q J
♣ J 5 2

The original opener showed 12–14 so South will now have a good 13–14.

You lead the four of hearts to the five, ten and queen. South now plays the ace and another diamond, your queen being allowed to hold as partner follows with the two and eight. You now play the ace of hearts on which dummy discards a club, partner following with the eight and declarer the seven. How do you continue and would it make any difference if East's second heart were the three?

Solutions:

Hand No. 16
You have the option to allow partner's nine of diamonds to hold or overtake and conduct the subsequent defence. The magic question surrounds the whereabouts of the two of clubs. West has indicated an original four-card suit by his three spot on the second round so it appears that South has hidden the two in an attempt to make the defenders believe that a ruff and discard is threatened. You, yourself, know that but West cannot be sure as you would have led back the four from A 10 8 4 2. You must overtake and continue clubs, forcing dummy to use its entry prematurely. The diamonds now cannot be enjoyed. If West had played high the second time, you would know he started with five (almost certainly) and must again overtake and attack spades hoping for a strong holding with West.

The deal:

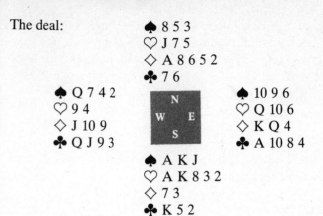

```
                        ♠ 8 5 3
                        ♡ J 7 5
                        ◇ A 8 6 5 2
                        ♣ 7 6
        ♠ Q 7 4 2          N          ♠ 10 9 6
        ♡ 9 4                          ♡ Q 10 6
        ◇ J 10 9      W        E       ◇ K Q 4
        ♣ Q J 9 3          S          ♣ A 10 8 4
                        ♠ A K J
                        ♡ A K 8 3 2
                        ◇ 7 3
                        ♣ K 5 2
```

Hand No. 17

Here the crucial question is whether the hearts will now run. Partner is giving you an ammeter signal that he has only two cards left and therefore, the next lead must come from him. (Had he started with J 10 x, he must, of course, unblock.) With the diamonds now established, South is threatening to run home with dummy's long suit and spades. You should consequently hope that partner has the ace of clubs and switch to clubs, the five being probably the best card.

If partner plays the three of hearts, you know that he started with four and can cash hearts from the top, defeating the contract even if South has the ace of clubs:

The deal:

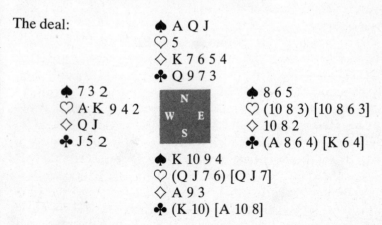

```
                        ♠ A Q J
                        ♡ 5
                        ◇ K 7 6 5 4
                        ♣ Q 9 7 3
        ♠ 7 3 2            N          ♠ 8 6 5
        ♡ A K 9 4 2                    ♡ (10 8 3) [10 8 6 3]
        ◇ Q J         W        E       ◇ 10 8 2
        ♣ J 5 2            S          ♣ (A 8 6 4) [K 6 4]
                        ♠ K 10 9 4
                        ♡ (Q J 7 6) [Q J 7]
                        ◇ A 9 3
                        ♣ (K 10) [A 10 8]
```

The other signal, almost invariably given by East to West, is the act of deliberately delaying the return of partner's suit to illustrate that your original holding was only a doubleton and that partner should take this into account when planning his subsequent defence; this normally occurs at no-trumps. An appropriate name for this signal might be:

THE FEBRUARY CHRISTMAS CARD
An example will illustrate the idea:

Hand No. 18
Dealer West
E–W Vulnerable

W	N	E	S
Pass	1♡	Pass	1NT
Pass	2NT	Pass	3NT
end			

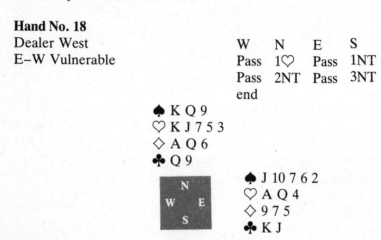

♠ K Q 9
♡ K J 7 5 3
◇ A Q 6
♣ Q 9

♠ J 10 7 6 2
♡ A Q 4
◇ 9 7 5
♣ K J

West leads the three of clubs to the queen, king and four; plan your defence.

Twenty-eight points are on view and with South likely to have about eight, partner is left with about four. The crucial card is the ace of clubs. If it is with South, then partner will have his values in spades or diamonds. These will be badly placed and you are unlikely to defeat the contract. It is therefore suggested that you consider the situation in which partner has the ace of clubs. If his clubs are as good as A 10 8 x x, you can cash out immediately. If not, you will have to be more careful. Even if South turns up with a five-card diamond suit, he will only have eight tricks on top. You can thus be fairly sure that he will have to attack hearts at some stage. In that event, you can take two heart tricks and three club tricks provided partner has A 10 x x or better, but he will need to overtake.

There is no way he will realise this if you play the jack of clubs at trick two. You should, therefore, exit passively in spades or diamonds, wait for hearts to be played, cash both your honours and only then lead the jack of clubs. Partner will then see that five tricks are available by overtaking.

The deal:

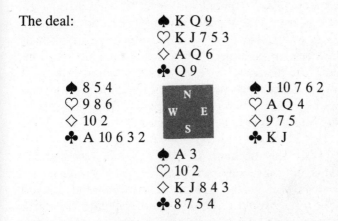

```
              ♠ K Q 9
              ♡ K J 7 5 3
              ◇ A Q 6
              ♣ Q 9
 ♠ 8 5 4              ♠ J 10 7 6 2
 ♡ 9 8 6        N     ♡ A Q 4
 ◇ 10 2     W     E   ◇ 9 7 5
 ♣ A 10 6 3 2   S     ♣ K J
              ♠ A 3
              ♡ 10 2
              ◇ K J 8 4 3
              ♣ 8 7 5 4
```

Having mastered the idea, you should have little difficulty in finding the correct defence here:

Hand No. 19
Dealer West
N–S Vulnerable

W	N	E	S
Pass	1♣	Pass	1◇
Pass	1♡	Pass	2NT
Pass	3NT	end	

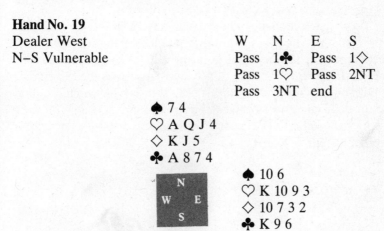

```
              ♠ 7 4
              ♡ A Q J 4
              ◇ K J 5
              ♣ A 8 7 4
                     ♠ 10 6
              N      ♡ K 10 9 3
           W     E   ◇ 10 7 3 2
              S      ♣ K 9 6
```

Partner leads the three of spades to the four, ten and king. South, who showed 11–12 points, leads the five of hearts to the two and dummy's jack; plan your defence.

With partner having indicated a trebleton, it is unlikely that you will gain by holding up. Furthermore, it may be dangerous to do so in that declarer will now have secured his second heart trick without losing the lead and may be able to switch suits to establish tricks outside. You should therefore take this trick but how do you follow?

This is a convenient moment to offer a little guide on roll-calling. The general rule is that, if you want to be optimistic about defeating a hand and can visualise a finesse position which is right for declarer, assume that the finessable card is in the South hand. The diamonds here are a case in point. If partner has the queen, declarer has no choice but to play him for it (you can see the ten so there is no two-way guess). Thus you should assume that South has the queen of diamonds.

Continuing the points roll-call on that assumption, you will probably realise that he must also have the ace of diamonds otherwise his first play would surely have been to knock it out. That makes six points and the king of spades already played increases the total to nine. The bidding and lead mark West with five spades and South four. Now let's roll-call the spade honours. With ♠ A Q J x x, it is likely that West would have led the queen and it appears, therefore, that South has the queen of spades leaving partner with the queen of clubs.

If you lead the spade back immediately, West will probably try to cash out (he does not know the distribution) presenting declarer with his ninth trick in the process. A better defence is to hope that partner has the ten of clubs as well as the queen and that you can set up two club tricks; you should switch to a low club. You cannot be prevented from coming in again with your king after which the February Christmas card of the six of spades will ensure five tricks.

The deal:

```
                    ♠ 7 4
                    ♡ A Q J 4
                    ◇ K J 5
                    ♣ A 8 7 4
♠ A J 8 3 2                         ♠ 10 6
♡ 7 6 2            N                ♡ K 10 9 3
◇ 9 4          W       E            ◇ 10 7 3 2
♣ Q 10 2           S               ♣ K 9 6
                    ♠ K Q 9 5
                    ♡ 8 5
                    ◇ A Q 8 6
                    ♣ J 5 3
```

5. The World of Suit Preference

Choice is a killer –
particularly in the wardrobe.

We now turn to situations in which it is necessary to draw partner's attention to a particular suit in positions where there are two or three choices all of which, from his point of view, may be reasonable.

There are, in principle, three ways of directing partner's attention to a particular suit:

NATURAL DISCARDS:

a) A high card encourages and vice versa. You can, of course, agree to play it the other way round with the advantage of preserving your cards in the suit you want led but with the disadvantage that you may have to throw a necessary high card to discourage a suit you do not want led, possibly to declarer's advantage.

b) Rather than play high or low, you can agree to play odd (encouraging) and even. The pros and cons of this were explained in an earlier chapter and apply here in a similar manner.

McKENNEY OR LAVINTHAL DISCARDS:

Which name depends respectively on whether you come from the East or West side of the Atlantic. This implies discarding almost invariably from a suit you do not want led. A high card indicates the higher of the outstanding suits and vice versa, ignoring trumps or declarer's obvious long suit at no-trumps.

This is best illustrated by a couple of examples:

i) Hearts are trumps. Declarer draws trumps early in the play and one defender cannot follow all the rounds. Then:

a high club or high diamond would show interest in spades,
a low club or high spade would show interest in diamonds,
a low spade or low diamond would show interest in clubs.
ii) There are no trumps. Declarer attacks his long suit, clubs. If a defender cannot follow, then:
a high heart or high diamond would show interest in spades,
a high spade or low diamond would show interest in hearts,
a low spade or low heart would show interest in diamonds.

Notice the use of the expression 'show interest'; these signals should not necessarily demand the lead of the suit implied but are given rather as an aid to the seven roll-calls and this cannot be repeated too often. On many occasions, we use McKenney signals to 'encourage' a ridiculous suit in order to tell partner that we cannot help in the other where this latter point may be in doubt.

The obvious question arises regarding what is to happen if you can only afford to discard from the suit you want led; suppose you hold something like:

♠ A Q 9 7 4 2 ♡ 6 ◇ Q 7 5 ♣ Q 8 4

Before you have a chance to bid your spades, the opponents are in 4♡ with you on lead. You judge that a trump is the safest lead and declarer continues to draw them. You cannot indicate spades to partner in one breath and your best chance is to throw the ♠4 and hope that a third round of trumps will be drawn when you will follow with the ♠2. This cannot be for clubs as you would have discarded the ♠2 first. Had you wanted diamonds, your first discard would have been a higher spade. Partner should now realise your problem.

McKenney discards have a clear advantage over natural discards in no-trump contracts in that you need not discard from the suit in which you are hoping to make tricks. Against this, you have to discard from suits which may help declarer. The advantage in suit contracts is, in my opinion, more clear-cut. Against trump contracts, it is likely that most of your tricks will come from suits in which you are short. You can thus discard informatively from useless long suits.

REVOLVING DISCARDS:

These are similar to McKenney but the order is different. Imagine the suits arranged in order of rank round the clock thus: low ♣ high ♣ low ♦ high ♦ low ♥ high ♥ low ♠ high ♠ low ♣ high ♣ and round we go again.

Once more, we ignore trumps or declarer's obvious suit at no-trumps and the discard will indicate interest in the suit 'nearest' to the card played. Let's do our examples again:

i) Hearts are trumps. Then, discarding on hearts:
   a low club or high diamond indicates spades,
   a high club or low spade indicates diamonds,
   a high spade or low diamond indicates clubs.
ii) There are no trumps and declarer plays on clubs; then:
   a high heart or low diamond indicates spades,
   a high diamond or low spade indicates hearts,
   a high spade or low heart indicates diamonds.

There appears to be little to choose between McKenney and revolving as they are effectively saying the same thing in two different languages. However, McKenney might have a slight edge for one reason.

With the scoring system as it is, the majority of suit contracts tend to be played in the majors. That implies that the defenders will be concentrating on the lower ranking suits. Using McKenney, you will always be throwing low cards to indicate clubs, the least popular trump suit. With Revolving, you will often have to throw a high card in a major suit if you cannot spare a low diamond. You could, of course, combat this by playing reverse McKenney but that is a strain on the memory—better to play 'high for high'. To some extent, the fact that, in no-trump contracts, declarer will often be playing on a minor, will counterbalance the above consideration.

For the remainder of the book, it will be assumed that we have agreed on McKenney.

For completeness, we must agree on the handling of two-suit situations, e.g. trump contracts in which one side suit is cleared completely early in the play. At a late stage, squeeze considerations may seriously inhibit your discarding options. In that event, the discard of a high card in either of your suits shows interest in the higher ranking suit and vice versa. As practice makes perfect, let's do our two examples again:

i) Hearts are trumps and they are drawn early. Declarer plays on clubs leaving spades and diamonds as the two outstanding suits. Then:
a high spade or high diamond shows interest in spades,
a low spade or low diamond shows interest in diamonds.

ii) There are no trumps and clubs are played off early. Declarer attacks diamonds and the two majors are left as the outstanding suits. Then:
a high spade or high heart shows interest in spades,
a low spade or low heart shows interest in hearts.

For clarity, you should, as far as possible, discard from the suit in which you have no interest.

Most experts recommend that the suit-preference signal should be used in the following three situations:

a) Against suit contracts when the opening leader wins the first trick or two in a side suit and it is clearly ridiculous for him to continue that suit.

b) Against suit contracts when one defender gives the other a ruff and wishes to suggest to partner what to play afterwards, notably to get him/her back on play for another ruff.

c) Against no-trump contracts when a defender is establishing his suit and wants to tell his partner in which suit his entry lies.

For most players, that is the beginning and the end of it. The point implied in the introduction to the book was that these signals apply in far more situations and that it is the failure of many players to appreciate this point that has led to considerable losses in defence. Let us, however, start with three simple examples on the main themes:

Hand No. 20
Dealer South
E–W Vulnerable

W	N	E	S
			1NT
Pass	3NT	end	

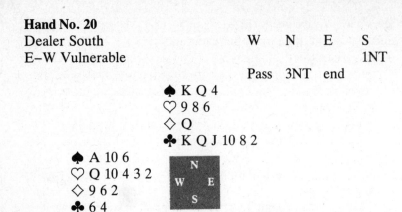

```
             ♠ K Q 4
             ♡ 9 8 6
             ◇ Q
             ♣ K Q J 10 8 2
  ♠ A 10 6        N
  ♡ Q 10 4 3 2  W   E
  ◇ 9 6 2         S
  ♣ 6 4
```

South's opener showed 12–14. You lead the three of hearts to the six, ace and five. Partner cashes the king of hearts and switches to the eight of spades. South plays the two; plan your defence.

Hand No. 21
Dealer East
N–S Vulnerable

W	N	E	S
		Pass	1♡
Pass	1♠	Pass	2NT
Pass	3♡	Pass	4♡
end			

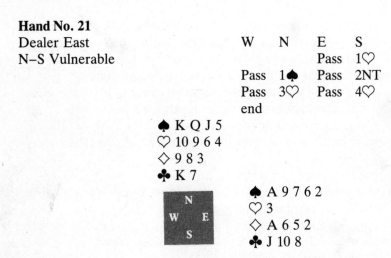

```
  ♠ K Q J 5
  ♡ 10 9 6 4
  ◇ 9 8 3
  ♣ K 7
         N          ♠ A 9 7 6 2
       W   E        ♡ 3
         S          ◇ A 6 5 2
                    ♣ J 10 8
```

After this straightforward Acol sequence in which South showed 17–18, partner leads the ten of spades and dummy's jack covers; plan your defence. Would it make any difference if your club and diamond holdings were reversed?

Hand No. 22

Dealer East
E–W Vulnerable

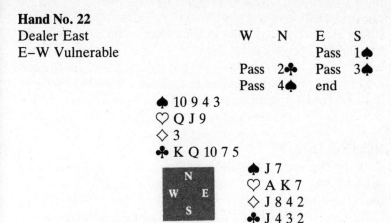

W	N	E	S
		Pass	1♠
Pass	2♣	Pass	3♠
Pass	4♠	end	

♠ 10 9 4 3
♡ Q J 9
◇ 3
♣ K Q 10 7 5

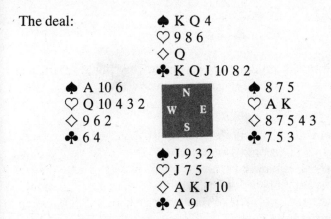

♠ J 7
♡ A K 7
◇ J 8 4 2
♣ J 4 3 2

Partner cashes the ace of clubs and switches to the six of hearts. Dummy plays the queen; plan your defence.

Solutions:

Hand No. 20

This is purely a matter of winning with the ace of spades and cashing the rest of the hearts for six tricks. You should have noticed that East played the top heart honours the wrong way round to indicate a doubleton.

The deal:

♠ K Q 4
♡ 9 8 6
◇ Q
♣ K Q J 10 8 2

♠ A 10 6
♡ Q 10 4 3 2
◇ 9 6 2
♣ 6 4

♠ 8 7 5
♡ A K
◇ 8 7 5 4 3
♣ 7 5 3

♠ J 9 3 2
♡ J 7 5
◇ A K J 10
♣ A 9

Now, which card did you play to trick two? Once partner indicated that doubleton heart, you should have appreciated his

83

problem of how to get you in so that you could cash the suit before declarer runs home in the minors. Your second heart should have been the ten to indicate a spade. Clubs are out of the reckoning as South will play them anyway so if you have the ace, it can wait. So it is a question of spades or diamonds and you must CLEARLY indicate which. The four could be misunderstood if South has falsecarded.

Hand No. 21
Most of the minor suit cards will clearly be well placed for declarer and you are not therefore going to defeat this contract unless that ten of spades is singleton. You should thus win and return the suit, choosing the nine to suggest the ace of diamonds as your reentry for the second ruff.

The deal:

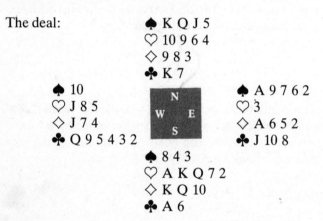

```
              ♠ K Q J 5
              ♡ 10 9 6 4
              ◇ 9 8 3
              ♣ K 7
♠ 10                              ♠ A 9 7 6 2
♡ J 8 5          N               ♡ 3
◇ J 7 4       W     E            ◇ A 6 5 2
♣ Q 9 5 4 3 2      S             ♣ J 10 8
              ♠ 8 4 3
              ♡ A K Q 7 2
              ◇ K Q 10
              ♣ A 6
```

If your minor suit holdings are reversed, you should return the two of spades to indicate the ace of clubs.

Hand No. 22
Here again with the clubs easily establishable, you are unlikely to defeat this hand unless that ace is a singleton. You should realise that this is almost certain. Partner will have little reason to lead from a suit bid over him unless this is the case. You should thus win with the king of hearts and return a high club requesting a further heart from partner.

The deal:

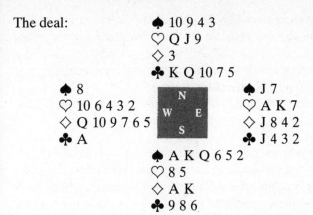

```
                    ♠ 10 9 4 3
                    ♡ Q J 9
                    ◇ 3
                    ♣ K Q 10 7 5
   ♠ 8                              ♠ J 7
   ♡ 10 6 4 3 2        N            ♡ A K 7
   ◇ Q 10 9 7 6 5   W     E         ◇ J 8 4 2
   ♣ A                 S            ♣ J 4 3 2
                    ♠ A K Q 6 5 2
                    ♡ 8 5
                    ◇ A K
                    ♣ 9 8 6
```

Now, which club did you play on trick one? This is a good example to illustrate that generosity pays. Realising that the ace was a sure singleton, you should have clearly indicated your entry by playing the jack. The mean defender who considers the four high enough could easily mislead his partner. South, holding 6 3 2 could follow with the six and now West sits there wondering whether his partner started with J 9 8 4 and is asking for a diamond or whether the deal is as above. How often does experience show that if you can possibly give a partner a chance to go wrong, rest assured he will! The play of the jack of clubs at trick one ensures an impregnable position for you in the postmortem.

Having seen the general idea, we can now proceed to discuss one or two problems with this system:

a) What happens if you want partner to continue his suit despite a singleton on dummy?

b) How are you to signal if your reentry for a second ruff is the ace of trumps and you cannot sit back and wait for trumps to be drawn, there being a danger that declarer will discard the suit to be ruffed on another side suit?

The accepted practice in these two cases is to treat the original or trump suit as a middle ranking suit irrespective of which suit it actually is, i.e. try to deny interest in the other two. If you have no middle ranking cards, for example a holding like 10 9 3 2, then try to suggest a suit that looks ridiculous and hope partner realises what is wanted.

We can now add two more situations for the use of the McKenney signal to add to the three we discussed above:

d) To indicate a devastating switch to partner which may not look right from his side of the table.
e) To help partner plan his discards in pseudo-squeeze situations.

It is the failure to use suit-preference signals in these two situations that seems to have caused many mishaps in top-class circles. Most notably, the pseudo-squeezes occur in high level contracts and now mistakes, particularly at rubber bridge or teams scoring, can be very expensive.

Hand No. 23
Dealer West
E–W Vulnerable

W	N	E	S
Pass	1NT	Pass	4♡
end			

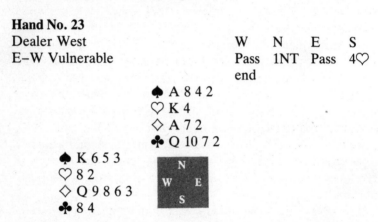

♠ A 8 4 2
♡ K 4
◇ A 7 2
♣ Q 10 7 2

♠ K 6 5 3
♡ 8 2
◇ Q 9 8 6 3
♣ 8 4

North's opener showed 12–14. You lead the eight of clubs to the two, jack and three. Partner cashes the ace and king of clubs and then plays the six. South ruffs high and draws trumps, partner following with the seven, five and three. Declarer continues trumps and you are forced to abandon one of your suits; plan your discards.

Hand No. 24
Dealer South
N–S Vulnerable

W	N	E	S
			1♠
Pass	2♡	3♣	Pass
Pass	3♠	Pass	4♠
end			

♠ K J 5
♡ K J 10 7 2
♢ K 4
♣ Q 6 2

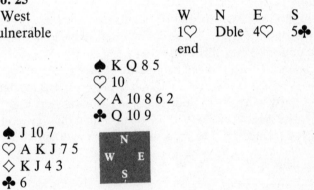

♠ A 7
♡ 6 5
♢ J 10 9
♣ A J 9 7 5 4

Partner leads the three of clubs to dummy's two; plan your defence.

Hand No. 25
Dealer West
N–S Vulnerable

W	N	E	S
1♡	Dble	4♡	5♣
end			

♠ K Q 8 5
♡ 10
♢ A 10 8 6 2
♣ Q 10 9

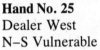

♠ J 10 7
♡ A K J 7 5
♢ K J 4 3
♣ 6

You lead the ace of hearts to the ten, six and four. How do you continue?

87

Hand No. 26
Dealer West
E–W Vulnerable

W	N	E	S
Pass	1♡	Pass	1NT
Pass	3NT	end	

♠ A Q 6
♡ Q J 10 4 3
♢ K Q
♣ A 10 9

♠ J 10 9 7 4
♡ A 6
♢ 9 6 4
♣ J 8 4

You lead the jack of spades to the ace, three and five. Dummy's ten of clubs is won by partner's king and he switches to the nine of hearts. South plays the seven; plan your defence.

Solutions:

Hand No. 23

You should have noticed two signals from partner.

Firstly, he played the ace of clubs before the king when he had the option to play them the other way round.

Secondly, he followed trumps down the line.

Both these signals clarified that his interest was in spades and you must hang on to your diamonds hoping that East has the ten—he is most unlikely to have more than that. He could have played trumps 7 3 5 to show mild interest in diamonds.

The deal:

♠ A 8 4 2
♡ K 4
♢ A 7 2
♣ Q 10 7 2

♠ K 6 5 3
♡ 8 2
♢ Q 9 8 6 3
♣ 8 4

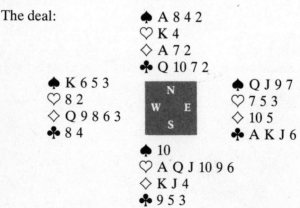

♠ Q J 9 7
♡ 7 5 3
♢ 10 5
♣ A K J 6

♠ 10
♡ A Q J 10 9 6
♢ K J 4
♣ 9 5 3

Hand No. 24

With both red kings apparently well placed, it is most unlikely that you will beat this contract unless that lead is a singleton. By way of confirmation, were West to hold ♣ K x x, a points roll-call would leave South with virtually everything else and in that case, eleven tricks are almost certain.

Thus you must win the first trick and return the suit, the question being which card. The seven looks the most non-committal and therefore the best to try and pinpoint the trump ace as your reentry.

The deal:

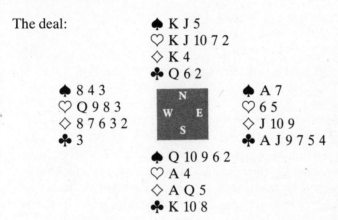

```
                    ♠ K J 5
                    ♡ K J 10 7 2
                    ◇ K 4
                    ♣ Q 6 2
   ♠ 8 4 3                        ♠ A 7
   ♡ Q 9 8 3          N           ♡ 6 5
   ◇ 8 7 6 3 2      W   E         ◇ J 10 9
   ♣ 3                S           ♣ A J 9 7 5 4
                    ♠ Q 10 9 6 2
                    ♡ A 4
                    ◇ A Q 5
                    ♣ K 10 8
```

Notice that, unless you take the two ruffs immediately, South can discard dummy's third club on diamonds before drawing trumps.

Hand No. 25

With partner having raised you to game, he is likely to have several hearts to choose from when following to the first trick. The six does not look particularly high or low. A roll-call on the trump suit completes the picture. Dummy has only three and although there is no law limiting South's holding, he certainly does not need to have more than five to justify his bidding. That leaves partner with four and if they include the king, he will desperately want to have one of dummy's trumps removed. You should therefore persist with the king of hearts.

The deal:
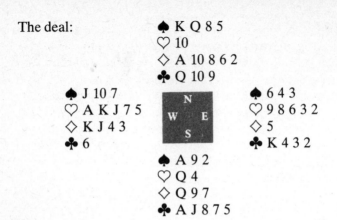

```
                    ♠ K Q 8 5
                    ♡ 10
                    ◇ A 10 8 6 2
                    ♣ Q 10 9
♠ J 10 7                              ♠ 6 4 3
♡ A K J 7 5         N                ♡ 9 8 6 3 2
◇ K J 4 3        W     E              ◇ 5
♣ 6                 S                ♣ K 4 3 2
                    ♠ A 9 2
                    ♡ Q 4
                    ◇ Q 9 7
                    ♣ A J 8 7 5
```

Note that, had East held poor trumps but a void of diamonds, the two would have been his first card.

Hand No. 26

Here, the first card to roll-call is the two of spades followed closely by the king of hearts. South's insistence on playing on a tenuous club suit as opposed to a solid heart suit with plenty of entries cries out for the magic question. Surely, if South held the king of hearts, his first assignment would have been to knock out your ace. As he didn't, the king must be with East. Yet, East returned the nine of hearts denying interest in the suit—thus implying interest elsewhere. Had he wanted diamonds, he could have played them himself. His failure to do so indicates that he wants you to play the suit in question and that can only be spades. Thus East started with K 3 2 and was in difficulties on trick one.

It will be a useful exercise to complete our seven roll-calls on these assumptions:

Spades:	We have established that East has K 3 2 and South 8 5.
Hearts:	East must have the king and nine and South two or three small.
Clubs:	South has the queen and probably two or more others.
Points:	South promised about 6–8 and therefore must have the ace of diamonds.

Diamonds:	We noticed that South does not appear to need the queen of clubs as entry to diamonds despite the blockage. This implies that he has the jack and ten and probably more.
Declarer's tricks:	We can now see what is happening. South is hoping to pinch a trick in clubs before running home in diamonds. He has one spade trick and two clubs so that gives him no less than six diamonds.
Defenders' tricks:	These must be taken now and will be two in each major and the king of clubs.

You must therefore take your ace of hearts and switch back to the ten of spades.

The deal:

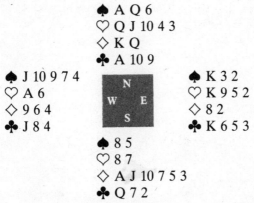

```
                    ♠ A Q 6
                    ♡ Q J 10 4 3
                    ◇ K Q
                    ♣ A 10 9
  ♠ J 10 9 7 4                      ♠ K 3 2
  ♡ A 6            N                ♡ K 9 5 2
  ◇ 9 6 4      W       E            ◇ 8 2
  ♣ J 8 4          S                ♣ K 6 5 3
                    ♠ 8 5
                    ♡ 8 7
                    ◇ A J 10 7 5 3
                    ♣ Q 7 2
```

You did, of course, drop the jack of clubs under the king to inform partner of where your entry lay—or did you leave him wondering whether South had Q J to a string of clubs and you perhaps had a diamond holding. Arguably, he could work it out but you certainly would have taken a great strain off him, which is what defensive signalling is all about.

Two more hands will illustrate the handling of a couple of other problems associated with this signalling system:

 i) the three-suit entry position,
ii) the McKenney–attitude paradox.

Hand No. 27
Dealer North
Game all

W	N	E	S
	Pass	Pass	1NT
Pass	2♣	Pass	2◇
Pass	2NT	Pass	3NT
	end		

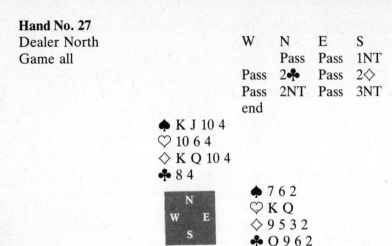

♠ K J 10 4
♡ 10 6 4
◇ K Q 10 4
♣ 8 4

♠ 7 6 2
♡ K Q
◇ 9 5 3 2
♣ Q 9 6 2

South's opener showed 15–17. Partner leads the five of hearts to the four, queen and three. On your king of hearts, South plays the eight, West the seven and North the six. How do you continue?

Hand No. 28
Dealer West
E–W Vulnerable

W	N	E	S
Pass	1◇	Pass	1♡
Pass	4♡	end	

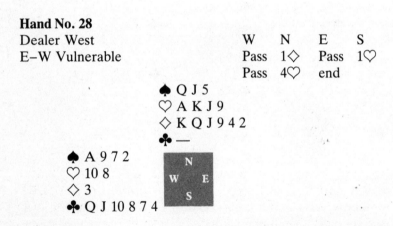

♠ Q J 5
♡ A K J 9
◇ K Q J 9 4 2
♣ —

♠ A 9 7 2
♡ 10 8
◇ 3
♣ Q J 10 8 7 4

You lead the three of diamonds to the jack, ace and six. East returns the ten of diamonds, South plays the eight and you ruff. How do you continue?

Solutions:

Hand No. 27
First of all, if there is to be any chance at all of defeating this contract, partner will have to have started with ♡ A x x x x and the suit will have to be brought in now. Too many cards are sitting right for declarer for there to be any other hope.

Roll-calling the heart suit in more detail on that assumption, you can place South with J 8 3 as West could have overtaken with A J x x x. This gives West A 9 7 5 2 and he has played the middle card of his three remaining low ones.

The middle of the three remaining suits is diamonds and a roll-call on declarer's tricks indicates that if partner has the diamond ace, it may not be safe to sit back and wait for declarer to play the suit. A points roll-call gives South exactly 16 and his raise to game could be based on a five-card club suit. That means he could take nine tricks in the black suits unless you switch to diamonds immediately.

The deal:

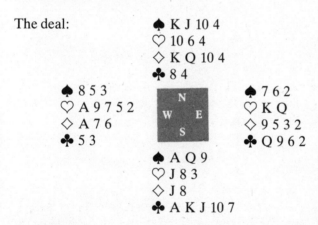

                ♠ K J 10 4
                ♡ 10 6 4
                ◇ K Q 10 4
                ♣ 8 4

    ♠ 8 5 3   ♠ 7 6 2
    ♡ A 9 7 5 2   ♡ K Q
    ◇ A 7 6   ◇ 9 5 3 2
    ♣ 5 3   ♣ Q 9 6 2

                ♠ A Q 9
                ♡ J 8 3
                ◇ J 8
                ♣ A K J 10 7

Hand No. 28
Partner's high diamond return indicates spades as his reentry suit but which spade are you going to lead? At the moment, you don't know the diamond split and whether another ruff is available. Your partner does know the split but if he has a four-card suit, he too will not know whether another ruff is available but for a different reason. He does not know if you have the queen of hearts.

You could lead the ace of spades now but that risks cutting the communication if South has a singleton. So it is a question of the nine or the two and you can now see the paradox:

On the attitude principle, the high card would deny interest in the suit and therefore request another diamond, clubs being out of the reckoning.

On the McKenney principle, the high card would show interest in the higher ranking suit and therefore request a spade return.

It is the usual practice in these situations for the attitude principle to be ruling. You should therefore lead the two of spades. Partner will still give you the second diamond ruff if he started with a trebleton but with four, he will know that you have denied the queen of trumps and simply return a spade.

Had you had the queen of trumps, you would have played the nine of spades, guaranteeing the ability to ruff.

The deal:

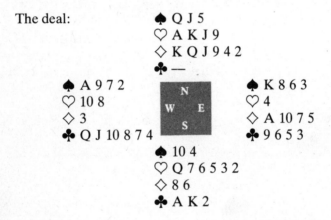

♠ Q J 5
♡ A K J 9
♢ K Q J 9 4 2
♣ —

♠ A 9 7 2　　　　　　　♠ K 8 6 3
♡ 10 8　　　　　　　　♡ 4
♢ 3　　　　　　　　　　♢ A 10 7 5
♣ Q J 10 8 7 4　　　　♣ 9 6 5 3

♠ 10 4
♡ Q 7 6 5 3 2
♢ 8 6
♣ A K 2

Strangely, had diamonds and spades been reversed in this deal, the attitude and McKenney principles would have been in harmony.

The paradox rears its ugly face again in connection with another suit-preference signal:

THE SMITH PETER

This normally occurs at no-trump contracts in which West has led a suit, say fourth highest, to an honour in the East hand which has lost to South. The question arises whether it is safe for him to lead the suit again, another honour being still at large.

Let us illustrate the problem with a couple of examples:

```
                    x x x
     A 10 x x x                   J x (Q J x)
                    K Q x (K x)
```

Here West leads his fourth card to the jack and king. South attacks his own suit losing to West. West does not know whether to continue his original suit.

Similarly here:

```
                    x x
     K x x x x                    10 x x (J 10 x)
                    A Q J (A Q x)
```

Again West leads his fourth to the ten and queen. When he gets the lead early, he does not know whether another round is safe.

There are a number of situations of this kind. The Smith peter is used to sort them out. The procedure is for East to play a high card on the trick West wins if he wants the original suit continued and vice versa. Sadly, where the original suit led is of low rank, the paradox strikes again. Here too, it is usual for the Smith peter to take precedence over McKenney.

Try a couple of problems, noting that the roles can be reversed:

Hand No. 29
Dealer North
Game All

W	N	E	S
	1♣	Pass	1♠
Pass	2♣	Pass	2NT
Pass	3NT	end	

♠ K
♡ J 10 7
◇ 10 8 5
♣ A K Q 10 9 3

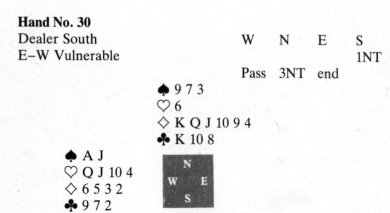

♠ 7 6 3 2
♡ A 9 6 5 2
◇ Q 4 3
♣ 8

South showed 11–12. Partner leads the two of diamonds to the five, queen and ace. South plays the five of spades. Partner wins and switches to the four of hearts on which dummy plays the seven; plan your defence.

Hand No. 30
Dealer South
E–W Vulnerable

W	N	E	S
			1NT
Pass	3NT	end	

♠ 9 7 3
♡ 6
◇ K Q J 10 9 4
♣ K 10 8

♠ A J
♡ Q J 10 4
◇ 6 5 3 2
♣ 9 7 2

South's opener showed 13–15. You lead the queen of hearts to the six, two and king. South plays the three of clubs to the king and partner's ace. East switches to the five of spades on which South plays the two and you win. How do you continue?

Solutions:

Hand No. 29

South's bidding suggested a stopper in hearts so it is clear that West has led the suit purely to get you in. This can only be for the purpose of returning his original suit and you should thus take your ace of hearts and switch back to the four of diamonds.

The deal:

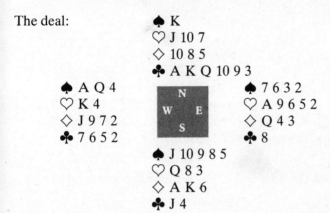

```
                    ♠ K
                    ♡ J 10 7
                    ◇ 10 8 5
                    ♣ A K Q 10 9 3
   ♠ A Q 4                          ♠ 7 6 3 2
   ♡ K 4              N             ♡ A 9 6 5 2
   ◇ J 9 7 2      W       E         ◇ Q 4 3
   ♣ 7 6 5 2          S            ♣ 8
                    ♠ J 10 9 8 5
                    ♡ Q 8 3
                    ◇ A K 6
                    ♣ J 4
```

Now, which card did you play to that spade trick? It should have been the two. The important message is that you cannot help if partner leads another diamond. Had you started with K Q x in the suit, your spade would have been the seven. Your count or attitude to the spade suit is of no interest to partner on this hand.

Hand No. 30

The first point you should have noticed is that South did not touch that wonderful diamond suit, clearly indicating that he has the ace. He also has a heart trick in the bag and your partner's discouragement indicates that South has another one. That accounts for eleven of his points and he is likely to have some strength in clubs. Thus you will defeat the contract now or never and you must obviously return your partner's suit i.e. the JACK of spades; you did, of course, win the first trick with the ace!

The deal:

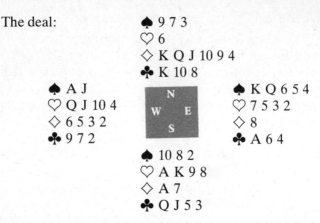

```
                    ♠ 9 7 3
                    ♡ 6
                    ◇ K Q J 10 9 4
                    ♣ K 10 8
♠ A J                             ♠ K Q 6 5 4
♡ Q J 10 4          N            ♡ 7 5 3 2
◇ 6 5 3 2        W     E         ◇ 8
♣ 9 7 2             S            ♣ A 6 4
                    ♠ 10 8 2
                    ♡ A K 9 8
                    ◇ A 7
                    ♣ Q J 5 3
```

Now, which card did you play on that club? It should have been
the two to indicate to partner that a continuation of hearts would
not be good enough. Had you started with:

♠ J ♡ A Q J 10 4 ◇ 6 5 3 2 ♣ 9 7 2 you would have played
the nine of clubs to encourage a continuation of your original
suit, hearts.

It has been assumed above that the Smith peter applies equally
to East and West. Some pairs play it the other way round for
West in that, if the leader peters, he is suggesting a switch and
vice versa. Authorities seem to be divided on this point.
Although there seems to be an advantage in that it normally will
be expected that West will want his partner to return his original
lead and therefore, more often than not, West will want to play a
low card, thus saving his high ones, it is suggested that, for
consistency and ease of memory, both players should play one
way.

To conclude the chapter, there are a number of variations,
each of which has advantages and disadvantages already
covered:

DODD DISCARDS

Here, a discard of an even card encourages that suit while an odd
card asks for the other suit of the same colour. Peter if you do not
hold a card of the required parity.

DUNSBY DISCARDS

A discard of an even card asks for the minor suit of the opposite colour. A discard of an odd card asks for the major suit of the opposite colour. You could, of course, agree to play it the other way round.

FINCH DISCARDS

A discard of an even card asks for the higher of the two other suits while an odd card suggests the lower.

TEXAS DISCARDS

A discard in one suit asks for the next higher ranking suit. Spades implies clubs, and trumps or declarer's long suit at no-trumps are excluded. The higher the discard, the stronger the message.

6. The Captain's Privilege

*There must be one to command
And one to obey.*

One of the greatest assets a defender can have is the ability to foresee the way a contract might be beaten and conduct the defence in such a way that his partner, who may know much less about the hand, cannot go wrong. The appreciation of when to take command and when to be led, as the situation warrants, is the principal booster to partnership morale and is therefore beyond value.

Try the following examples, noting in each case that there may be something that you know which your partner doesn't. Attempt to anticipate any problems he may have to face and try to arrange that he doesn't go wrong.

Hand No. 31
Dealer North
E–W Vulnerable

W	N	E	S
	1♦	Pass	1♡
Pass	2♡	Pass	4♡
end			

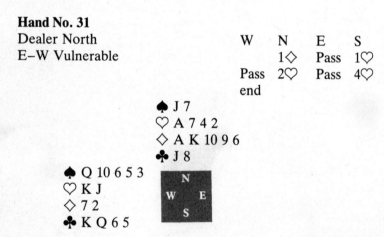

```
              ♠ J 7
              ♡ A 7 4 2
              ◇ A K 10 9 6
              ♣ J 8
♠ Q 10 6 5 3      N
♡ K J          W     E
◇ 7 2             S
♣ K Q 6 5
```

You lead the king of clubs to the eight, seven and four. How do you continue?

Hand No. 32
Dealer South
Game all

W	N	E	S
			4♠

end

♠ Q 8 3
♡ K Q J
♢ 9 7 5
♣ K J 6 3

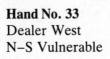

♠ —
♡ 10 8 7 4
♢ J 3
♣ A Q 8 7 5 4 2

Partner leads the ten of clubs to dummy's three; plan your defence.

Hand No. 33
Dealer West
N–S Vulnerable

W	N	E	S
Pass	1♢	1♡	1♠
2♡	Dble	Pass	3♠

end

♠ Q J 10
♡ J 4
♢ A Q J 9 6
♣ K Q 9

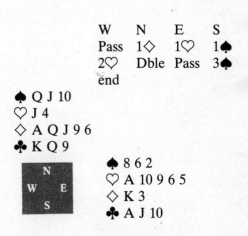

♠ 8 6 2
♡ A 10 9 6 5
♢ K 3
♣ A J 10

North's double was competitive. Partner leads the king of hearts to dummy's four; plan your defence.

Solutions:

Hand No. 31

You should have realised two points on this hand. Firstly, you know that you are going to make a trump trick whereas partner does not. Secondly, the spade situation is potentially dangerous. If South has both top honours, there is nothing to discuss. Even if he has only one, two rounds of clubs will have to stand up if you are to have any chance.

You can now visualise the danger if partner has the ace of spades. If he wins the second club, then unaware of your trump trick, he may feel obliged to push a low spade through to give South a guess. South will go up (that is his only hope if a trump has to be lost) and make the contract. To avoid putting partner in this position, you should play the queen of clubs at trick two clarifying that you wish to hold the trick. After that, you can switch to spades and partner is now forced to play his ace.

The deal:

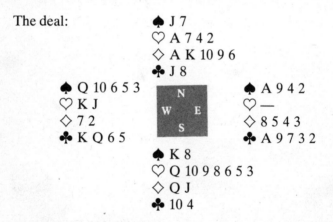

```
                    ♠ J 7
                    ♡ A 7 4 2
                    ◇ A K 10 9 6
                    ♣ J 8
    ♠ Q 10 6 5 3         N          ♠ A 9 4 2
    ♡ K J                           ♡ —
    ◇ 7 2         W        E        ◇ 8 5 4 3
    ♣ K Q 6 5         S              ♣ A 9 7 3 2
                    ♠ K 8
                    ♡ Q 10 9 8 6 5 3
                    ◇ Q J
                    ♣ 10 4
```

Hand No. 32

Unless the first round of clubs stands up, you are probably not going to beat this contract so should work on the assumption that it does. Any tricks available to the defenders in the majors are unlikely to run away so you should turn your attention to diamonds.

If partner has two of the top three, it is unlikely to matter which card you play. The critical position arises where partner has ace and ten and declarer king and queen. If you now lead the

102

jack, South will cover and West cannot enjoy two tricks in the suit whether he wins or ducks. However, if you lead the three, West will be able to continue the attack on taking his ace.

All this assumes that you win trick one. Notice that South, aware of the diamond danger, did not cover the ten of clubs. In the situation where you held the ace of hearts, it would be difficult for West to underlead his diamonds, the necessary defence in that event.

You should take charge by playing the queen of clubs on trick one and switching to the three of diamonds:

The deal:

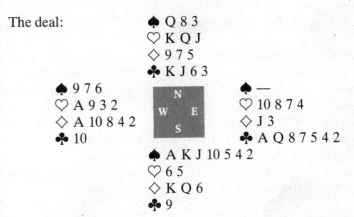

```
                    ♠ Q 8 3
                    ♡ K Q J
                    ◇ 9 7 5
                    ♣ K J 6 3
      ♠ 9 7 6                      ♠ —
      ♡ A 9 3 2        N           ♡ 10 8 7 4
      ◇ A 10 8 4 2   W   E         ◇ J 3
      ♣ 10             S           ♣ A Q 8 7 5 4 2
                    ♠ A K J 10 5 4 2
                    ♡ 6 5
                    ◇ K Q 6
                    ♣ 9
```

Hand No. 33

A points roll-call will indicate that partner has the two heart honours and nothing else. That means that, if you are to make five tricks, both red suits will have to go round twice and you will have to set up two club tricks immediately. You could play a discouraging five of hearts and partner ought to realise that he will need to lead clubs through twice and switch immediately, retaining his queen of hearts as entry.

But why force partner to work things out when you can do the work yourself? Just overtake in hearts and switch to the jack of clubs. When you are given your king of diamonds, you will then underlead your hearts and partner, now fully aware of what is happening, cannot go wrong.

The deal:

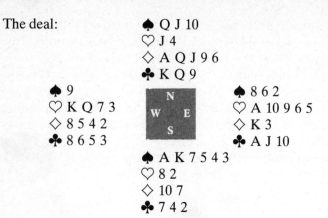

♠ Q J 10
♥ J 4
♦ A Q J 9 6
♣ K Q 9

♠ 9
♥ K Q 7 3
♦ 8 5 4 2
♣ 8 6 5 3

♠ 8 6 2
♥ A 10 9 6 5
♦ K 3
♣ A J 10

♠ A K 7 5 4 3
♥ 8 2
♦ 10 7
♣ 7 4 2

It is possible that partner has led from K x x x in hearts from his very poor hand in order to stay on lead as he knows the North hand is strong. But in that case, you cannot organise two club tricks and all you will have done is to give away an overtrick for everyone to laugh about afterwards!

You will have seen on all these hands how life was made easy for partner.

Having grasped the idea, you should be able to solve two more examples with little difficulty:

Hand No. 34
Dealer East
N–S Vulnerable

W	N	E	S
		Pass	1NT
Pass	2♦	Pass	2♥
Pass	3♣	Pass	3♠
Pass	4♦	Pass	5♥
Pass	6♥	end	

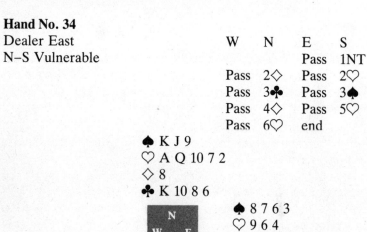

♠ K J 9
♥ A Q 10 7 2
♦ 8
♣ K 10 8 6

♠ 8 7 6 3
♥ 9 6 4
♦ A 10 2
♣ Q 7 2

South's opener showed 13–15. North transferred to hearts and then showed his club suit. South's 3♠ showed that he had values in spades but could not stop diamonds. North now had a problem. 3NT was now out of the question so all he could do was to bid the fourth suit asking partner to bid game in hearts or clubs. In the meantime, South had actually meant his 3♠ to be an advanced cue-bid, intending to support hearts afterwards. Reading the 4◇ bid to be a likely control, he invited a slam and North, with all his points clearly working, accepted.

Partner leads the king of diamonds to dummy's eight; plan your defence.

Hand No. 35
Dealer East
E–W Vulnerable

W	N	E	S
		Pass	1NT
Pass	2♣	Pass	2♠
Pass	4♠	end	

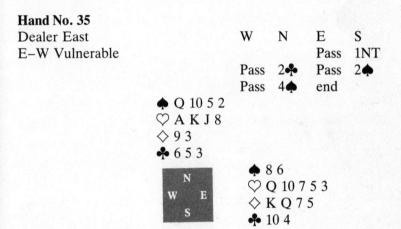

♠ Q 10 5 2
♡ A K J 8
◇ 9 3
♣ 6 5 3

♠ 8 6
♡ Q 10 7 5 3
◇ K Q 7 5
♣ 10 4

South's opener showed 15–17. Partner leads the jack of diamonds to dummy's three; plan your defence.

Solutions:

Hand No. 34
You have an awkward card to play on this trick. With the opponents having crawled up to a slam with a possible misunderstanding, passive defence must be in order. Partner should, of course, realise this but if you play the ten or two, he might think you are crying out for a switch. As the black suits shouldn't be touched with a bargepole, your best line is to overtake the diamond and switch to a trump leaving declarer to play the hand.

The deal:

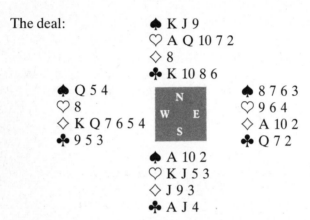

```
                    ♠ K J 9
                    ♡ A Q 10 7 2
                    ◇ 8
                    ♣ K 10 8 6
   ♠ Q 5 4                          ♠ 8 7 6 3
   ♡ 8              N               ♡ 9 6 4
   ◇ K Q 7 6 5 4  W   E             ◇ A 10 2
   ♣ 9 5 3          S               ♣ Q 7 2
                    ♠ A 10 2
                    ♡ K J 5 3
                    ◇ J 9 3
                    ♣ A J 4
```

Hand No. 35
The important thing to realise here is that you know the heart suit on dummy cannot be established but your partner doesn't. You also know that, because of the heart position, South will have to go for ruffs in the minors on dummy. The defence, therefore, should be to attack trumps and this is best done from your side of the table, particularly if partner has an honour. You can see the danger. If you play low on trick one, South can duck leaving partner on play and he may well go wrong. You should insist that any diamond trick will be won in your hand so that you can switch to trumps. You should thus play the queen of diamonds now.

The deal:

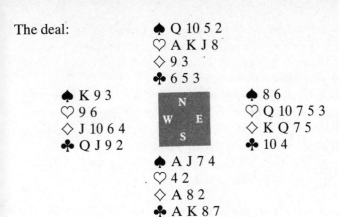

If South takes your queen and returns the suit, partner should realise what is happening and keep his ten so that declarer's eight is not set up.

Continuing the idea of alerting partner at every possible opportunity, we shall now introduce two further signals:

THE FOGHORN

This is normally the play, cashing or discarding an apparently ridiculous card, usually unnecessarily high, to alert partner that you have the contract beaten and you want him/her to work out how. Often a ruff is involved or some unusual situation. The foghorn tells you that there is something up and declarer is going crashing. What would you make of this?

Hand No. 36
Dealer East
Love all

W	N	E	S
		Pass	1♡
Pass	4♡	end	

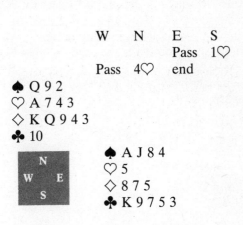

Partner leads the ace of diamonds to the three, five, and two. He switches to the three of spades to the two, jack and five. You cash your ace of spades drawing the seven from South and partner drops the king. How do you continue?

The foghorn card is the king of spades. Without it, you would be wondering whether a third trick in the suit is available. Partner has told you that something is 'on' and as that can only be a diamond ruff, you should return a diamond.

The deal:

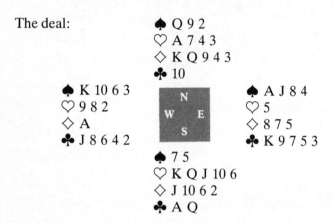

```
                    ♠ Q 9 2
                    ♡ A 7 4 3
                    ◇ K Q 9 4 3
                    ♣ 10
  ♠ K 10 6 3                        ♠ A J 8 4
  ♡ 9 8 2          N               ♡ 5
  ◇ A           W     E            ◇ 8 7 5
  ♣ J 8 6 4 2       S               ♣ K 9 7 5 3
                    ♠ 7 5
                    ♡ K Q J 10 6
                    ◇ J 10 6 2
                    ♣ A Q
```

An interesting point arises regarding which spade West should lead at trick two. On the attitude principle, a low card implies interest in the suit whereas he desperately wants a switch back to diamonds. Against that, were he to lead the ten, you may well duck leaving him on play which again West does not want. Are you going to realise that a diamond is needed on winning the second round of spades with no idea of the count in that suit?

Having seen the idea, you can now give a few foghorn signals yourself. Remember, partner cannot see your hand and may not know as much about the full deal as you do. It is then your duty to alert him.

Hand No. 37
Dealer West
E–W Vulnerable

W	N	E	S
Pass	Pass	Pass	2NT
Pass	3NT	end	

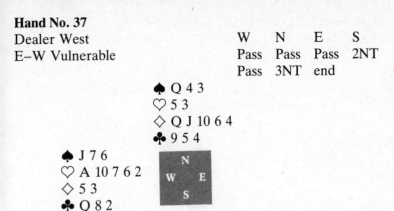

♠ Q 4 3
♡ 5 3
◇ Q J 10 6 4
♣ 9 5 4

♠ J 7 6
♡ A 10 7 6 2
◇ 5 3
♣ Q 8 2

South's opener showed 20–22. You lead the six of hearts to the three, queen and king. South now cashes the ace and king of diamonds. You follow with the five and three and partner with the seven and two. Now South plays the king of spades. Partner wins and returns the nine of hearts to South's four; plan your defence.

Hand No. 38
Dealer East
Game all

W	N	E	S
		Pass	Pass
Pass	2◇	Pass	2♡
Pass	3NT	Pass	4◇
Pass	4♡	end	

♠ A Q J
♡ K Q J 9
◇ A K
♣ K Q J 5

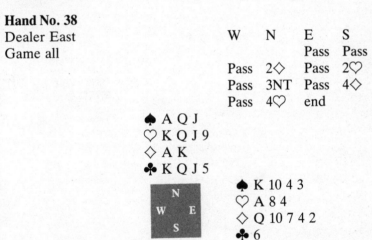

♠ K 10 4 3
♡ A 8 4
◇ Q 10 7 4 2
♣ 6

This was a Benjaminised Acol sequence in which North showed 24–26 balanced but because of the Herbert negative, the hand unfortunately had to be declared by the weak partner, the transfer coming too late.

Partner leads the eight of spades to the jack, king and two. How do you continue?

Hand No. 39
Dealer South
Game all

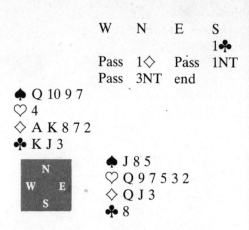

W	N	E	S
			1♣
Pass	1◇	Pass	1NT
Pass	3NT	end	

♠ Q 10 9 7
♡ 4
◇ A K 8 7 2
♣ K J 3

♠ J 8 5
♡ Q 9 7 5 3 2
◇ Q J 3
♣ 8

Your opponents are playing a strong no-trump in this position so South will hold about 12–14 points. Partner leads the six of hearts to the four, queen and ace. Crossing to the table with a diamond honour, South calls for the ten of spades. 'Cover an honour with an honour!' they say. Do you consider that wise on this occasion?

Hand No. 40
Dealer West
N–S Vulnerable

W	N	E	S
Pass	1♣	Pass	2NT
Pass	3NT	end	

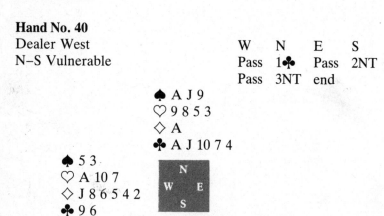

♠ A J 9
♡ 9 8 5 3
◇ A
♣ A J 10 7 4

♠ 5 3
♡ A 10 7
◇ J 8 6 5 4 2
♣ 9 6

South showed 11–12. You lead the five of diamonds to the ace, ten and seven. South now runs the queen of spades to partner's king. East cashes the king of diamonds, South playing the nine and switches to the six of hearts. South plays the four and your ten wins. How do you continue?

110

Solutions:

Hand No. 37

This could hardly be easier. With the queen of spades having become an entry, you can see that the diamonds on dummy will all make. You will therefore defeat the contract now or never. Either let the nine of hearts hold, East will need a third one anyway, or overtake with the ten and cash out from the top:

The deal:

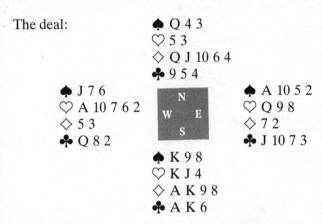

```
                    ♠ Q 4 3
                    ♡ 5 3
                    ♢ Q J 10 6 4
                    ♣ 9 5 4
  ♠ J 7 6                          ♠ A 10 5 2
  ♡ A 10 7 6 2                     ♡ Q 9 8
  ♢ 5 3                            ♢ 7 2
  ♣ Q 8 2                          ♣ J 10 7 3
                    ♠ K 9 8
                    ♡ K J 4
                    ♢ A K 9 8
                    ♣ A K 6
```

Now, which card did you play under that king of spades? The foghorn card is the jack. Declarer has either two diamonds or four. If it is only two, partner should duck the king of spades. Did you look at those diamond pips carefully? Had the ace and king been a doubleton, East will have started with 9 8 7 2 and would surely have managed something higher on the first round. Partner should have been thinking similarly when he saw your 5 and 3. It is likely that South was trying to give the wrong impression when he cashed the two tops and switched, trying to look a player who couldn't get to dummy. It is up to you to direct partner to the right defence.

Hand No. 38

With the enormous hand on dummy (well, it wouldn't be dealt to you, would it?) and South having promised at least five hearts, you can see that partner will have to have the ace of clubs if there is to be any chance. Equally, partner will know that he will need to find you with the trump ace. You can thus see that a club ruff will set the contract immediately . . . but partner can't!

If you lead a club back now, he should read you for a doubleton and duck the first round expecting you to play the second one when you get in with the trump ace. The foghorn card is, therefore, an immediate ace of trumps. Then switch to the club and partner cannot go wrong.

The deal:

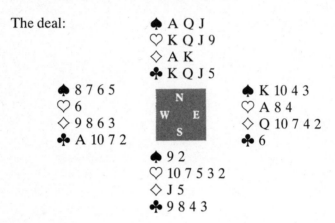

Alternatively, though less clear, you might exit passively in spades or diamonds now and switch to the club when in with the trump ace.

Hand No. 39
Assuming that West has led from a four-card suit, you see that you can defeat this contract in hearts alone but partner may not realise this. He knows that you do not have the jack and if he hasn't got it either, he may sit with his king waiting for a lead from your side. With the nine of spades on view, it would be ridiculous to cover the ten. If South has either the ace or king but not both, you will save him a two-way guess; but that is considering the spade suit on its own. In the context of the whole hand, the jack of spades is the foghorn card. If you play low, declarer may well run it and West might duck. Even if he wins, how can he know whether South started with two hearts or three (and that assumes his bidding has denied four—by no means certain —some players deny majors when it is likely they are heading for 3NT)? By playing the jack of spades now, you make it clear to partner that there is no other hope but hearts.

The deal:

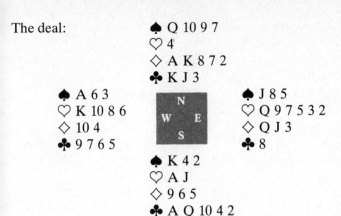

♠ Q 10 9 7
♥ 4
♦ A K 8 7 2
♣ K J 3

♠ A 6 3
♥ K 10 8 6
♦ 10 4
♣ 9 7 6 5

♠ J 8 5
♥ Q 9 7 5 3 2
♦ Q J 3
♣ 8

♠ K 4 2
♥ A J
♦ 9 6 5
♣ A Q 10 4 2

And which card did you play under the diamond honour at trick two? There are not many hands where there is an opportunity to give two foghorn signals but this is one of them. You should have dropped an honour, preferably the queen. Once you see the heart position, you should try and shout at partner at every possible opportunity.

Hand No. 40

You should have noted a number of factors.

Firstly, South failed to bid spades and yet started playing them rather than clubs. The implication is that he has the clubs already set up.

Secondly, the three of diamonds has not appeared.

Thirdly, the fact that you were allowed a trick with the ten of hearts suggests that South has only one honour and East two.

Completing a points roll-call on those assumptions, you can see that South started with the king and queen of clubs, the queen of diamonds and the king or queen of hearts. If it is the king, partner would have led the queen from Q J 6, so clearly he has K J 6. You should thus continue hearts to complete five tricks.

The deal:

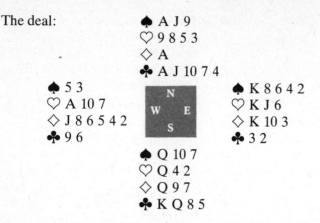

```
                    ♠ A J 9
                    ♡ 9 8 5 3
                    ◇ A
                    ♣ A J 10 7 4
   ♠ 5 3                            ♠ K 8 6 4 2
   ♡ A 10 7          N              ♡ K J 6
   ◇ J 8 6 5 4 2   W   E            ◇ K 10 3
   ♣ 9 6             S              ♣ 3 2
                    ♠ Q 10 7
                    ♡ Q 4 2
                    ◇ Q 9 7
                    ♣ K Q 8 5
```

Now, which card did you play under that king of diamonds? How did partner know that he had to switch to hearts? The foghorn card is the jack. This denies the queen and clarifies to partner that continuing diamonds will not be good enough.

We are now beginning to see how vital it is to watch partner's cards and make use of the information given. The idea of treating a signal as a command, be it positive or negative, should be well out of your system by this stage.

We now include a rare situation in which a defender can prevent his partner from making the 'usual' play.

THE EMERGENCY CALL
999 of course! This signal is used to locate a missing nine in a situation where it matters.

Hand No. 41
Dealer East
E-W Vulnerable

W	N	E	S
		Pass	1♠
Pass	4♠	end	

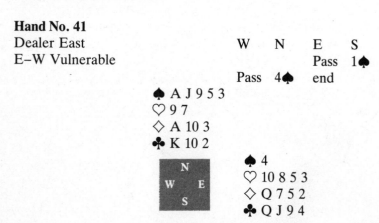

```
   ♠ A J 9 5 3
   ♡ 9 7
   ◇ A 10 3
   ♣ K 10 2
                    ♠ 4
        N           ♡ 10 8 5 3
     W     E        ◇ Q 7 5 2
        S           ♣ Q J 9 4
```

114

South's opener showed a five-card suit and 11–15.

Partner leads the ace and king of hearts, bringing down the queen and jack from South. West now switches to a trump and South takes two rounds ending in dummy. Now follow three rounds of clubs and you have to win the third.

How do you continue if partner's clubs were 3 7 8?

Would it make any difference if he had played 3 8 7?

It is clear that South must have the king of diamonds if he is to have any chance. Therefore, West must have the jack if the defence is to have any hope at all. The crucial card is the nine. If South has it, your only chance is to play the queen of diamonds and hope that South plays you for Q J x (x). He should play for split honours if he considers probabilities in the light of the principle of restricted choice. But particularly if he does not consider you a first-class player, he might decide that it is unlikely that you would lead the queen from nothing and go down as a result.

On the other hand, should West have the nine, then the play of a low diamond ensures declarer's doom. So which is it to be? The answer lies in partner's following to the clubs. If he plays in the usual order, up the line, he has nothing to say and you must play the queen of diamonds and hope. But if he plays them in an unusual order, within the discipline of showing an odd number of clubs, then you must assume that he HAS got something to tell you and that can only be that he has the nine of diamonds. Now you should play a low diamond.

The deal:

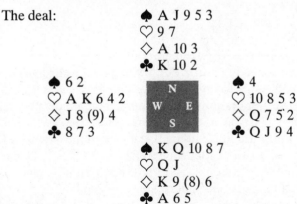

```
                    ♠ A J 9 5 3
                    ♡ 9 7
                    ◇ A 10 3
                    ♣ K 10 2
  ♠ 6 2                              ♠ 4
  ♡ A K 6 4 2          N            ♡ 10 8 5 3
  ◇ J 8 (9) 4      W       E        ◇ Q 7 5 2
  ♣ 8 7 3              S            ♣ Q J 9 4
                    ♠ K Q 10 8 7
                    ♡ Q J
                    ◇ K 9 (8) 6
                    ♣ A 6 5
```

This is a low-key version of the foghorn signal.

7. *The Sphere of Deception*

Little girls who tell lies don't go to Heaven.
But with modern day morals, those who tell the
truth CERTAINLY don't go to Heaven.

Deception is like a circular saw—a very necessary but very dangerous tool which must be used with extreme caution. Most importantly, a deceptive defence designed to fool declarer but actually fooling partner is one of the worst misdemeanours in the game if only for the long-term damage to partnership confidence.

It is for that reason that the following advice regarding the deliberate play of false cards might be fitting:

1) Note that deception falls into two categories—that intended to mislead
    a) declarer,
    b) partner.
2) Avoid deception unless you are fairly sure that it is the only reasonable hope of defeating the contract.
3) The most probable time for anti-declarer deception arises when partner obviously has a very poor hand and that, consequently, it will not matter if he roll-calls the deal incorrectly.
4) Deception of partner will normally be necessary if you know enough about the hand to be sure that he will follow the wrong line were you to defend naturally.
5) If you feel a deception is in order, try to plan it well ahead so that, when the crunch comes, your deceptive card is played at normal speed. Hesitation may be deemed an unethical help to partner or an unfair trick on declarer. Note, however, that in the East position, it is not unethical to plan the defence of the whole hand before following to trick one. If you have a singleton or obvious card to play to the opening lead, place it face down until your calculations are completed.
6) Most important, if you do go in for deception and partner is fatally fooled, make sure that YOU take the blame even if

you can, by deep analysis, demonstrate that he could have
worked it out. If you try to shift the responsibility, partner
will be hopelessly torn as regarding trust of your future
signals and the loss will now be incalculable.

Bearing the above in mind, try your sleight of hand on the
following:

Hand No. 42

	W	N	E	S
Dealer East			Pass	1NT
Game all	Pass	3NT	end	

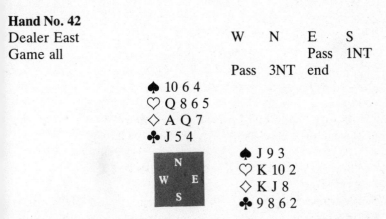

♠ 10 6 4
♡ Q 8 6 5
◇ A Q 7
♣ J 5 4

♠ J 9 3
♡ K 10 2
◇ K J 8
♣ 9 8 6 2

South's opener showed 16–18. Partner leads the seven of spades
to the four, nine and king. South now plays the three of clubs to
the ten and jack; plan your defence.

Hand No. 43

	W	N	E	S
Dealer South				1♣
E–W Vulnerable	Pass	1♠	Pass	2NT
	end			

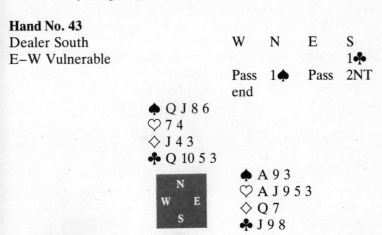

♠ Q J 8 6
♡ 7 4
◇ J 4 3
♣ Q 10 5 3

♠ A 9 3
♡ A J 9 5 3
◇ Q 7
♣ J 9 8

South showed 17–18. Partner leads the ten of diamonds and

declarer wins in hand with the ace, dummy having played low. South follows with the ace and two of clubs, partner's king winning the second round. West switches to the six of hearts and dummy plays the four; plan your defence.

Hand No. 44
Dealer East
E–W Vulnerable

W	N	E	S
		Pass	1NT
Pass	2♣	Pass	2♠
end			

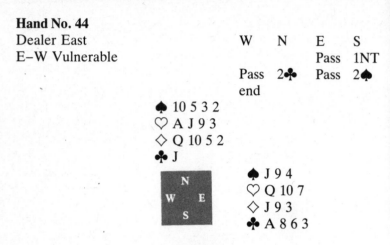

♠ 10 5 3 2
♡ A J 9 3
♢ Q 10 5 2
♣ J

♠ J 9 4
♡ Q 10 7
♢ J 9 3
♣ A 8 6 3

South's opener showed 12–14. Partner leads the ace of diamonds followed by the king. He continues with the seven of diamonds and South tries the ten. You win with the jack, South still following. How do you continue?

Hand No. 45
Dealer East
Love all

W	N	E	S
		Pass	1NT
Pass	3NT	end	

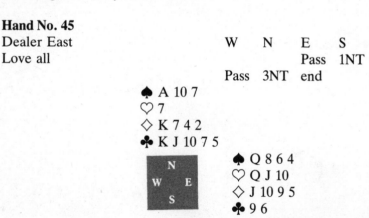

♠ A 10 7
♡ 7
♢ K 7 4 2
♣ K J 10 7 5

♠ Q 8 6 4
♡ Q J 10
♢ J 10 9 5
♣ 9 6

South's opener showed 13–15. Partner leads the four of hearts and you are allowed to win the first two tricks, partner playing the two on the second round and South the three and five. South

wins the third round with the ace and leads the four of clubs to
partner's ace and dummy's five. Which card do you play?

Solutions:

Hand No. 42
Quick roll-calling is needed here otherwise you will be caught.
Partner's lead of the seven and declarer's king indicate that the
spades are now ready to cash. The ten of clubs looks very much
like a singleton which gives South five tricks in the suit. That, in
addition to the spade, makes six and the points roll-call marks
South with the ace of hearts and he may well also have the jack.
The two red aces put the enemy total up to eight tricks and a red
suit finesse would make nine.

If the jack of hearts is with West, South has no sensible option
but to take the diamond finesse, going down, but it may be that
he has that jack in which case it will cost nothing to try the queen
of hearts in case anything happens before committing himself to
the diamond. It is up to you to be ready to play low on the queen
of hearts without a flicker.

The deal:

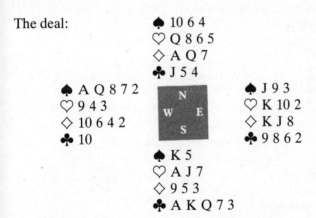

```
                    ♠ 10 6 4
                    ♡ Q 8 6 5
                    ◇ A Q 7
                    ♣ J 5 4
   ♠ A Q 8 7 2                      ♠ J 9 3
   ♡ 9 4 3          N               ♡ K 10 2
   ◇ 10 6 4 2     W   E             ◇ K J 8
   ♣ 10             S               ♣ 9 8 6 2
                    ♠ K 5
                    ♡ A J 7
                    ◇ 9 5 3
                    ♣ A K Q 7 3
```

Hand No. 43
Partner has done well to find your suit but you will still need to
find him with one of the honours if the defence is to have a
chance. You may well get away with playing ace and another as
long as partner unblocks. South can duck the second round but
you still have the ace of spades as entry. Far better, however, is

to play the jack of hearts now, so keeping lines of communication easily open.

The deal:

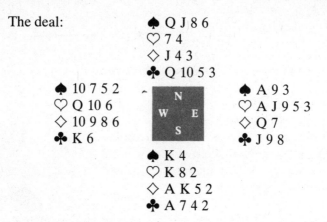

```
              ♠ Q J 8 6
              ♡ 7 4
              ◇ J 4 3
              ♣ Q 10 5 3
♠ 10 7 5 2                      ♠ A 9 3
♡ Q 10 6         N             ♡ A J 9 5 3
◇ 10 9 8 6    W     E          ◇ Q 7
♣ K 6            S             ♣ J 9 8
              ♠ K 4
              ♡ K 8 2
              ◇ A K 5 2
              ♣ A 7 4 2
```

Now, which card did you play to trick one? Or, to put it another way, how did partner know that he had to switch away from diamonds? You should have tossed in the queen even though dummy's jack was not played to clarify to partner that the position in the suit was hopeless. The seven would almost certainly be misread.

Hand No. 44
A return of any side suit card other than a low club will give the defence a chance to defeat the contract but the point of interest is how you played to the first two tricks. This is an ideal situation for a false peter, the nine followed by the three. South may well take the view that the third round will be ruffed and that he should preserve dummy's queen of diamonds to save himself the heart finesse. After stealing the third diamond, the defenders will take their ace of clubs and unless declarer plays against the odds, two trump tricks.

The deal:

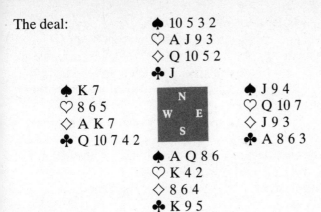

```
              ♠ 10 5 3 2
              ♡ A J 9 3
              ◇ Q 10 5 2
              ♣ J
♠ K 7                          ♠ J 9 4
♡ 8 6 5          N             ♡ Q 10 7
◇ A K 7       W     E          ◇ J 9 3
♣ Q 10 7 4 2     S             ♣ A 8 6 3
              ♠ A Q 8 6
              ♡ K 4 2
              ◇ 8 6 4
              ♣ K 9 5
```

Hand No. 45

Which card you play to this trick is of no consequence—what matters is how you played to tricks one and two. The natural order is the ten and then the queen but if you did that, South would know the position of the jack and could win the SECOND round of hearts, blocking the suit. Your best play, therefore, is the jack followed by the queen. If you tried the jack and then the ten, South could see that you had done something strange and might save the day. The recommended order gives nothing away to declarer and represents the best chance of avoiding the block.

The deal:

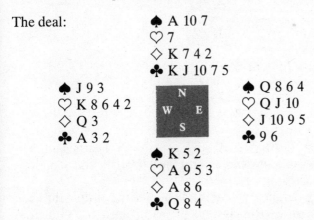

```
              ♠ A 10 7
              ♡ 7
              ◇ K 7 4 2
              ♣ K J 10 7 5
♠ J 9 3                        ♠ Q 8 6 4
♡ K 8 6 4 2      N             ♡ Q J 10
◇ Q 3         W     E          ◇ J 10 9 5
♣ A 3 2          S             ♣ 9 6
              ♠ K 5 2
              ♡ A 9 5 3
              ◇ A 8 6
              ♣ Q 8 4
```

We now turn to a relatively new and ingenious invention which is an attempt to circumvent the principal disadvantage of all signalling—the fact that any signal to partner is also a signal to declarer.

ENCRYPTED SIGNALS

The principle here is that once declarer's count in a particular suit is known exactly, a complete count roll-call is available to both defenders but not to declarer. The defenders can therefore vary their signalling system according to their own count without declarer's knowledge.

The facility is likely to be available in at least two situations:

a) Where the auction indicated an exact length of one of South's suits.
b) Where South shows out of one suit very early in the play.

An example will illustrate the idea:

Hand No. 46
Dealer South
Love all

W	N	E	S
			2♡
Pass	4♡	end	

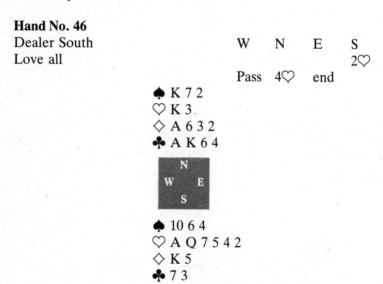

♠ K 7 2
♡ K 3
♢ A 6 3 2
♣ A K 6 4

♠ 10 6 4
♡ A Q 7 5 4 2
♢ K 5
♣ 7 3

Your opener showed 7–10 and exactly six hearts and that therefore becomes the code suit for the defenders who announce the following system:

If the defender on lead has an odd number of cards in the code suit, the system is: Roman honour leads, third and fifth from length, upside-down attitude and count signals.

If the defender on lead has an even number of cards in the code suit, the system is standard honour leads, fourth highest from length, standard attitude and count signals.

Now, how do you play on the lead of the jack of spades?

Cruel, isn't it? You could cover the jack only to find that this is the deal:

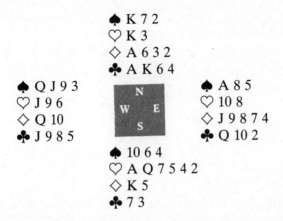

<pre>
            ♠ K 7 2
            ♡ K 3
            ◇ A 6 3 2
            ♣ A K 6 4
♠ Q J 9 3   ♠ A 8 5
♡ J 9 6   ♡ 10 8
◇ Q 10   ◇ J 9 8 7 4
♣ J 9 8 5   ♣ Q 10 2
            ♠ 10 6 4
            ♡ A Q 7 5 4 2
            ◇ K 5
            ♣ 7 3
</pre>

The defenders take three rounds of spades and a fourth round promotes a trump trick. On the other hand you could duck trick one, only to find to your horror that the deal is:

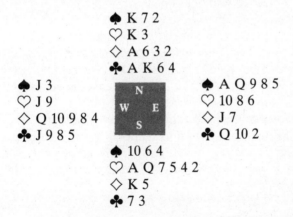

<pre>
            ♠ K 7 2
            ♡ K 3
            ◇ A 6 3 2
            ♣ A K 6 4
♠ J 3   ♠ A Q 9 8 5
♡ J 9   ♡ 10 8 6
◇ Q 10 9 8 4   ◇ J 7
♣ J 9 8 5   ♣ Q 10 2
            ♠ 10 6 4
            ♡ A Q 7 5 4 2
            ◇ K 5
            ♣ 7 3
</pre>

and now again after three top spades, a fourth round effects a trump promotion. In each case, had you played the other way round, you would have made the contract.

Nonetheless, it isn't all doom. We only have to alter the hand slightly and all of a sudden, the under-the-table whispers can turn sour on the defenders.

Assume the same conditions and auction as before:

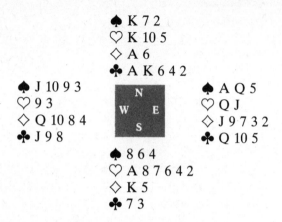

```
                    ♠ K 7 2
                    ♡ K 10 5
                    ◇ A 6
                    ♣ A K 6 4 2
♠ J 10 9 3                          ♠ A Q 5
♡ 9 3          N                    ♡ Q J
◇ Q 10 8 4   W   E                  ◇ J 9 7 3 2
♣ J 9 8          S                  ♣ Q 10 5
                    ♠ 8 6 4
                    ♡ A 8 7 6 4 2
                    ◇ K 5
                    ♣ 7 3
```

West leads the jack of spades and the defenders take their three tricks before exiting passively in diamonds. Now, when East follows to the ace of hearts, South, instead of playing for restricted choice, plays for the drop of the second heart honour. He knows that West has made a standard lead and therefore must have an even number of hearts.

Nonetheless, this method is bound, in the long term, to give a substantial advantage to the defending side.

This is neither time nor place to enter into the controversies of bridge politics but many players are likely to agree that at least a small question mark must be placed against the ethics of such a system.

In Section 4 of the proprieties, the laws state that:

'It is improper to convey information to partner by means of a call or play based on special partnership agreement, whether explicit or implicit, unless such information is freely available to the opponents.'

It will be for the authorities to decide whether this type of signal falls under that heading.

8. A Compendium Test

There is time for a hundred
visions and revisions.

Up to now, we have looked at the various methods of signalling under a number of headings. Therefore, in each problem set so far, you had a fair idea of what was wanted in that you realised which subject was under discussion.

We are now going to the table and in the examples which follow, you will have to decide which signal is appropriate and whether you should be giving or receiving it. Bear in mind that there is no guarantee that any signal will be needed at all!

We shall not be able to use all the systems in the world simultaneously as the playing of a given method excludes some of the others. Thus, in the problems that follow, you should assume the following:

1) We are playing standard honour leads, except Q from A K Q.
2) We use discretion when leading from three or more low cards.
3) The following signals may appear in the problems:
   a) Alarm clock lead
   b) Lone Ranger
   c) Bechgaard echo
   d) Six-shooter
   e) Ammeter
   f) February Christmas card
   g) Cash register
   h) Foghorn
   i) McKenney/Lavinthal
   j) Smith peter
   k) Emergency call
4) We play fourth high from four or more to an honour unless attitude considerations dictate otherwise.
5) The following will not appear:
   a) Non-standard lead styles including American and Trelde

b) The Vinje method, Scanian combination or REO rule

c) Wenceslaus signal, Foster echo, Encrypted signals

d) Natural, revolving, Dodd, Dunsby, Finch, or Texas discards.

6) The declarer is of top standard but also a fallible human being.

7) The bidding will be natural Acol style (unless carefully explained otherwise when full details will be given) and fairly accurate.

8) You are expected to do your seven roll-calls at every opportunity.

9) You are reminded again that you are not always asked for your play at the critical moment and you should state your play at every trick where it was not specifically stated; no credit otherwise.

Good luck!

Hand No. 47

Dealer West	♠ —
E–W Vulnerable	♡ 7 5 2
	◇ K 8 6 4 3
	♣ J 10 9 8 6

W	N	E	S
Pass	1NT	Pass	4♡
end			

North showed 13–15

What do you lead as West?

Hand No. 48

Dealer East	♠ A 7 5 3
N–S Vulnerable	♡ 10 8 5 2
	◇ 9 5
	♣ 8 7 5

W	N	E	S
		Pass	1◇
Pass	2♣	Pass	2♡
Pass	4◇	Pass	4♡
Pass	5♣	Pass	5◇
end			

What do you lead as West?

Hand No. 49

		W	N	E	S
Dealer South	♠ —				
E–W Vulnerable	♡ 9 4				Pass
	◇ A K J 10 9 6 3	3◇	Dble	Pass	4♣
	♣ 9 6 5 2	Pass	4◇	Pass	5♡
		Pass	6♡	end	

North's double was for take out and the cue bid showed majors with extra strength.

What do you lead as West?

Hand No. 50

		W	N	E	S
Dealer East	♠ K 5				
E–W Vulnerable	♡ 10 3 2			Pass	1♠
	◇ K 8 6 2	Pass	2♣	Pass	2◇
	♣ K 10 8 5	Pass	2♡	Pass	3♣
		Pass	3♠	Pass	4♠
		end			

What do you lead as West?

Hand No. 51

		W	N	E	S
Dealer East	♠ 10 4				
Love all	♡ 10 4 2			Pass	2NT
	◇ Q 5	Pass	3NT	end	
	♣ K Q 10 8 6 5				

♠ 6 2
♡ A J 8 7 5
◇ 10 9 6
♣ 9 3 2

```
      N
  W       E
      S
```

South's opener showed 20–22. You lead the seven of hearts to the two, queen and king. South leads the jack of clubs; plan your defence.

Solutions:

Hand No. 47
You have a solid club suit to lead from and it is normal to lead top of a sequence. But with that void of spades, your prime consideration is to get partner in. Were you to lead the jack, there is a danger that partner may sit with honours over North and you may be allowed to hold the trick, positively the last thing you want. It is therefore better to lead the ten or the nine.

The deal:

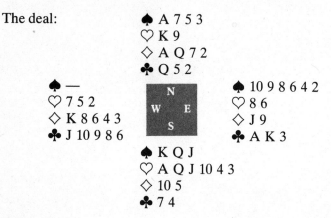

```
              ♠ A 7 5 3
              ♡ K 9
              ◇ A Q 7 2
              ♣ Q 5 2
♠ —                          ♠ 10 9 8 6 4 2
♡ 7 5 2           N          ♡ 8 6
◇ K 8 6 4 3   W       E      ◇ J 9
♣ J 10 9 8 6      S          ♣ A K 3
              ♠ K Q J
              ♡ A Q J 10 4 3
              ◇ 10 5
              ♣ 7 4
```

Hand No. 48
Here you obviously have to attack spades and the bidding indicates that North is very weak in the suit. You therefore gain nothing by leading the ace and it could well cost. The three is a better shot.

The deal:

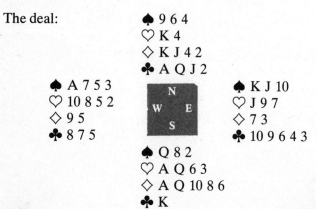

```
              ♠ 9 6 4
              ♡ K 4
              ◇ K J 4 2
              ♣ A Q J 2
♠ A 7 5 3                    ♠ K J 10
♡ 10 8 5 2        N          ♡ J 9 7
◇ 9 5        W       E       ◇ 7 3
♣ 8 7 5          S           ♣ 10 9 6 4 3
              ♠ Q 8 2
              ♡ A Q 6 3
              ◇ A Q 10 8 6
              ♣ K
```

128

Hand No. 49
The opposition have clearly got all the cards outside diamonds and you are unlikely to have any hope unless one round of your suit stands up. Your best chance, therefore, is to hope that partner holds the queen and North has bid the slam with a small singleton as his control. You should play the alarm clock lead of the ten or nine of diamonds suggesting spades as the return.

The deal:

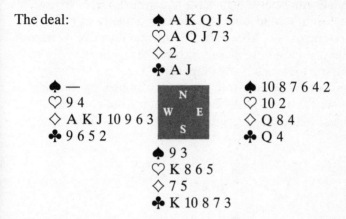

```
                  ♠ A K Q J 5
                  ♡ A Q J 7 3
                  ◇ 2
                  ♣ A J
    ♠ —                         ♠ 10 8 7 6 4 2
    ♡ 9 4             N         ♡ 10 2
    ◇ A K J 10 9 6 3  W   E     ◇ Q 8 4
    ♣ 9 6 5 2            S      ♣ Q 4
                  ♠ 9 3
                  ♡ K 8 6 5
                  ◇ 7 5
                  ♣ K 10 8 7 3
```

Hand No. 50
South appears to be 5 1 4 3 and it is likely that partner is sitting with honours over North. As the count is advertised, you should make the honour position clear by leading the ten of hearts. You can subsequently sit back and wait for a trick in each suit.

The deal:

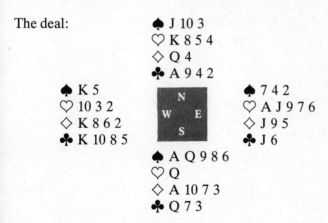

```
                  ♠ J 10 3
                  ♡ K 8 5 4
                  ◇ Q 4
                  ♣ A 9 4 2
    ♠ K 5                       ♠ 7 4 2
    ♡ 10 3 2          N         ♡ A J 9 7 6
    ◇ K 8 6 2     W       E     ◇ J 9 5
    ♣ K 10 8 5           S      ♣ J 6
                  ♠ A Q 9 8 6
                  ♡ Q
                  ◇ A 10 7 3
                  ♣ Q 7 3
```

129

Hand No. 51

East has almost certainly got the ace of clubs otherwise there is nothing to discuss. You are expected to give the count in this situation so that he knows how long to hold it up. But let us look deeper into the position. A points roll-call on that club assumption leaves partner with no more than a further queen which implies that the queen of diamonds is almost certainly an entry to dummy. Furthermore, you have the hearts ready to cash if partner has a second one and you are unlikely to defeat the contract if he hasn't. Above all, if South and East have two clubs each and you show a trebleton, East will duck, possibly allowing South to run for home in the other suits. You should take up the Captain's privilege and deceive partner by playing the nine of clubs now. There will then be little point in East's holding up (as he 'knows' South has a trebleton) and he should win and return a heart.

The deal:

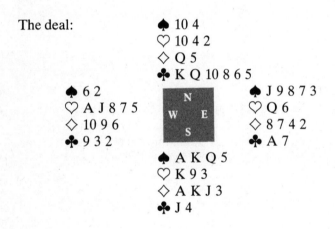

                        ♠ 10 4
                        ♡ 10 4 2
                        ♢ Q 5
                        ♣ K Q 10 8 6 5

♠ 6 2   ♠ J 9 8 7 3
♡ A J 8 7 5   ♡ Q 6
♢ 10 9 6   ♢ 8 7 4 2
♣ 9 3 2   ♣ A 7

                        ♠ A K Q 5
                        ♡ K 9 3
                        ♢ A K J 3
                        ♣ J 4

Hand No. 52
Dealer West
Love all

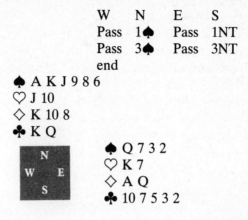

W	N	E	S
Pass	1♠	Pass	1NT
Pass	3♠	Pass	3NT
end			

♠ A K J 9 8 6
♡ J 10
◇ K 10 8
♣ K Q

♠ Q 7 3 2
♡ K 7
◇ A Q
♣ 10 7 5 3 2

Partner leads the five of hearts to the ten, king and three. How do you continue?

Hand No. 53
Dealer East
E–W Vulnerable

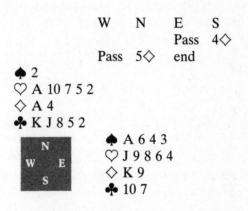

W	N	E	S
		Pass	4◇
Pass	5◇	end	

♠ 2
♡ A 10 7 5 2
◇ A 4
♣ K J 8 5 2

♠ A 6 4 3
♡ J 9 8 6 4
◇ K 9
♣ 10 7

Partner leads the king of spades to dummy's two; plan your defence.

131

Dealer East
Game all

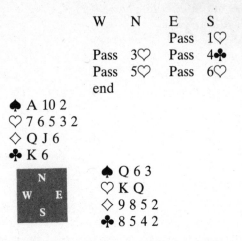

W	N	E	S
		Pass	1♡
Pass	3♡	Pass	4♣
Pass	5♡	Pass	6♡
end			

♠ A 10 2
♡ 7 6 5 3 2
♢ Q J 6
♣ K 6

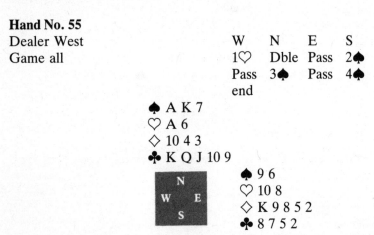

♠ Q 6 3
♡ K Q
♢ 9 8 5 2
♣ 8 5 4 2

Partner leads the queen of clubs. South wins in dummy and plays a trump to the queen and ace. Now follow the ace of clubs, partner playing the ten, and three top diamonds, partner following with the three, ten and seven. Having ended in dummy, South plays another trump which you win, partner following. How do you continue?

Hand No. 55
Dealer West
Game all

W	N	E	S
1♡	Dble	Pass	2♣
Pass	3♣	Pass	4♣
end			

♠ A K 7
♡ A 6
♢ 10 4 3
♣ K Q J 10 9

♠ 9 6
♡ 10 8
♢ K 9 8 5 2
♣ 8 7 5 2

Partner leads the ace of clubs. Taking the view that neither attitude towards clubs nor count in the suit are relevant, you play the two which clearly requests a diamond. Partner duly switches to the ace and then the six of diamonds, dummy playing low, you

132

the eight and king and South the seven and queen. How do you continue?

Hand No. 56
Dealer East
Love all

W	N	E	S
		Pass	1◇
2NT	3♡	Dble	5◇
	end		

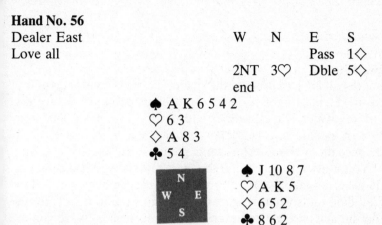

♠ A K 6 5 4 2
♡ 6 3
◇ A 8 3
♣ 5 4

♠ J 10 8 7
♡ A K 5
◇ 6 5 2
♣ 8 6 2

West's 2NT was unusual, showing at least 5–5 in the lowest outstanding suits, here clubs and hearts. Thus North's 3♡ was a cue-bid, showing interest in diamonds but offering spades as an alternative. Partner leads the queen of hearts and you overtake with the king and cash the ace. South follows with the two and nine. How do you continue if partner's second heart is: a) the ten; b) the four?

Hand No. 57
Dealer North
Game all

W	N	E	S
	Pass	2♡	2♠
	end		

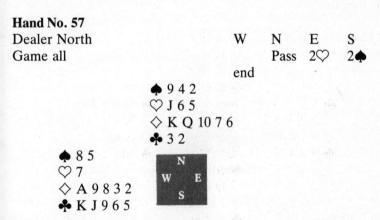

♠ 9 4 2
♡ J 6 5
◇ K Q 10 7 6
♣ 3 2

♠ 8 5
♡ 7
◇ A 9 8 3 2
♣ K J 9 6 5

East showed 7–10 and exactly six hearts. You lead the seven of hearts to the five, ace and three. Partner cashes the king of hearts on which you discard a low diamond and then the nine of hearts which you ruff, South having started with Q 10 3. How do you continue?

Solutions:

Hand No. 52
South will have to bring in the spade suit if this contract is going to make. He ought to have about eight points to justify his bidding which leaves partner with four at the most. That will clearly include one heart honour and if it is the queen, the defence has no hope as he cannot get in.

You must assume, therefore, that it is the ace and thus the defence can take five tricks provided West can be persuaded to lead diamonds when he gets in. You must see to it, therefore, that he does not get too excited about his hearts. Were you to return the suit immediately, he may well duck for lack of entries, hoping that you hold a third card in the suit. (Note that South should play the eight on the second round to help create that impression.)

This is an ideal position for a February Christmas card. Just return a passive seven of clubs now, wait till you get in with the queen of spades and only then return the heart. Partner will then realise why you have been so late in 'replying' and realise what he has to do.

The deal:

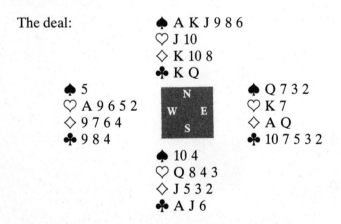

```
                    ♠ A K J 9 8 6
                    ♡ J 10
                    ◇ K 10 8
                    ♣ K Q
     ♠ 5                              ♠ Q 7 3 2
     ♡ A 9 6 5 2        N            ♡ K 7
     ◇ 9 7 6 4       W     E         ◇ A Q
     ♣ 9 8 4            S            ♣ 10 7 5 3 2
                    ♠ 10 4
                    ♡ Q 8 4 3
                    ◇ J 5 3 2
                    ♣ A J 6
```

Hand No. 53

You can see that one spade trick and one diamond trick will be available to the defence and the only realistic hope for a third is the ace of clubs with partner. The appearance of that tenace position in dummy spells danger. If South were to lead a club towards dummy at an early stage, West might well play low as he is ignorant of the trump position. In all seriousness, he should go up anyway but why give him the chance to go wrong? Just overtake the spade and lead a club yourself, forcing partner into the correct defence.

The deal:

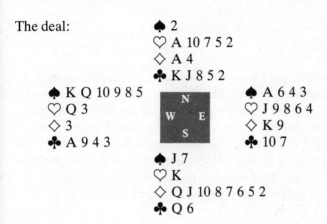

```
                    ♠ 2
                    ♡ A 10 7 5 2
                    ◇ A 4
                    ♣ K J 8 5 2
   ♠ K Q 10 9 8 5                   ♠ A 6 4 3
   ♡ Q 3              N             ♡ J 9 8 6 4
   ◇ 3            W       E         ◇ K 9
   ♣ A 9 4 3          S            ♣ 10 7
                    ♠ J 7
                    ♡ K
                    ◇ Q J 10 8 7 6 5 2
                    ♣ Q 6
```

Hand No. 54

Partner's ten of clubs was an ammeter indicating that he started with five and his strange order of following the diamonds can be nothing but an emergency call indicating the nine of spades. You should thus exit with a low spade. Had partner denied the nine, you would have had to try the queen and hope that declarer, thinking you are of the weaker brethren, plays you for both honours.

The deal:

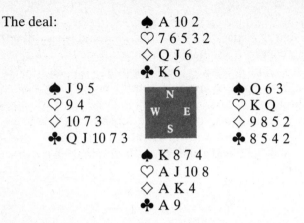

```
                    ♠ A 10 2
                    ♡ 7 6 5 3 2
                    ◇ Q J 6
                    ♣ K 6
♠ J 9 5                             ♠ Q 6 3
♡ 9 4              N                ♡ K Q
◇ 10 7 3        W     E             ◇ 9 8 5 2
♣ Q J 10 7 3       S               ♣ 8 5 4 2
                    ♠ K 8 7 4
                    ♡ A J 10 8
                    ◇ A K 4
                    ♣ A 9
```

Hand No. 55

Here you will be wondering which minor suit partner can ruff. If he had started with A x in both suits, it would have been a toss up which one to lead. On the principle of restricted choice, it appears that clubs is the more likely candidate. However, there is another point which swings the balance the other way. Had that club ace really been a singleton, why didn't West underlead his ace of diamonds to give you no chance to go wrong? There was certainly nothing to be gained by leading the ace first. You should thus continue diamonds.

The deal:

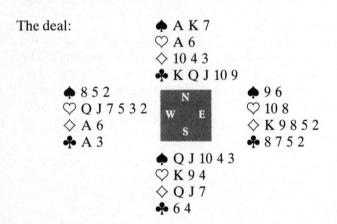

```
                    ♠ A K 7
                    ♡ A 6
                    ◇ 10 4 3
                    ♣ K Q J 10 9
♠ 8 5 2                            ♠ 9 6
♡ Q J 7 5 3 2      N               ♡ 10 8
◇ A 6           W     E            ◇ K 9 8 5 2
♣ A 3              S               ♣ 8 7 5 2
                    ♠ Q J 10 4 3
                    ♡ K 9 4
                    ◇ Q J 7
                    ♣ 6 4
```

Hand No. 56

By taking your heart honours in the normal order, you have shown your partner that you have at least one more and that the

136

option to force dummy is available. Partner's duty in this situation is to give his current count in hearts i.e. the ammeter. If he plays the ten of hearts indicating an original holding of five, you must force dummy with a third round to kill the spade suit. The ruffing entry then has to be used before it is needed. If partner plays low, indicating an original six-card suit, you will have no alternative but to switch to clubs, hoping to score the setting trick.

The deal:

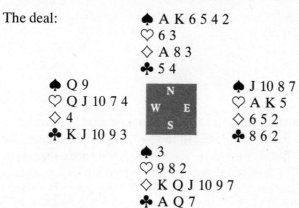

```
              ♠ A K 6 5 4 2
              ♡ 6 3
              ◇ A 8 3
              ♣ 5 4
♠ Q 9                        ♠ J 10 8 7
♡ Q J 10 7 4    N            ♡ A K 5
◇ 4          W     E         ◇ 6 5 2
♣ K J 10 9 3    S            ♣ 8 6 2
              ♠ 3
              ♡ 9 8 2
              ◇ K Q J 10 9 7
              ♣ A Q 7
```

Hand No. 57

Partner's unusual way of cashing his heart honours and his choice of a high one as the third cries out for the higher ranking minor and that can only be because he is void. He could have led a singleton himself. You should thus return a low diamond indicating a switch to clubs and at the same time, keeping control of diamonds by holding on to your ace.

The deal:

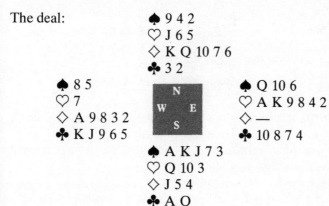

```
              ♠ 9 4 2
              ♡ J 6 5
              ◇ K Q 10 7 6
              ♣ 3 2
♠ 8 5                        ♠ Q 10 6
♡ 7           N              ♡ A K 9 8 4 2
◇ A 9 8 3 2  W     E         ◇ —
♣ K J 9 6 5     S            ♣ 10 8 7 4
              ♠ A K J 7 3
              ♡ Q 10 3
              ◇ J 5 4
              ♣ A Q
```

137

Hand No. 58
Dealer West

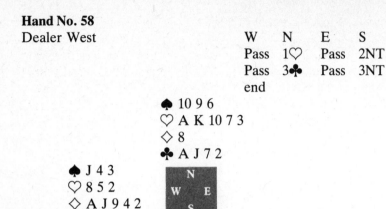

W	N	E	S
Pass	1♡	Pass	2NT
Pass	3♣	Pass	3NT
end			

```
              ♠ 10 9 6
              ♡ A K 10 7 3
              ◇ 8
              ♣ A J 7 2
♠ J 4 3        N
♡ 8 5 2     W     E
◇ A J 9 4 2    S
♣ 9 6
```

South showed 11–12. You lead the four of diamonds to the eight, king and five. Partner switches to the two of spades and South's king wins. He finesses the jack of hearts to your partner's queen and now East returns the three of diamonds to South's ten; plan your defence.

Hand No. 59
Dealer East
Game all

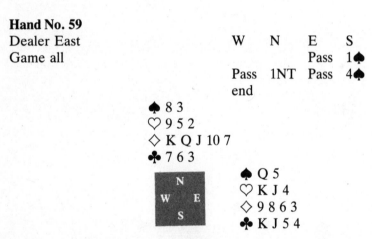

W	N	E	S
		Pass	1♠
Pass	1NT	Pass	4♠
end			

```
         ♠ 8 3
         ♡ 9 5 2
         ◇ K Q J 10 7
         ♣ 7 6 3
             N          ♠ Q 5
          W     E       ♡ K J 4
             S          ◇ 9 8 6 3
                        ♣ K J 5 4
```

Partner leads the six of hearts to the two, king and ace. South draws trumps bringing down the four and jack from partner. Now the five of diamonds goes to partner's ace and dummy's seven. Which card do you play?

Hand No. 60
Dealer South
E–W Vulnerable

W	N	E	S
			2♣
Pass	2♦	Pass	2♠
Pass	2NT	Pass	4♠
end			

♠ 4 2
♡ 10 8 7
♦ J 6 4
♣ J 8 6 4 3

♠ 9 5
♡ Q 6 5 4 3 2
♦ 10 8 5 2
♣ 9

Partner cashes the king, ace and queen of diamonds all following. He switches to a trump and South wins. A string of trumps follow, partner showing out on the third round. Plan your discards.

Solutions:

Hand No. 58
Partner's late return of your good suit is clear February Christmas card and you must cash both your diamonds before returning the spade to partner's ace for the setting trick. East kept his ace in case your diamonds were weaker and you started with Q x x in spades.

The deal:

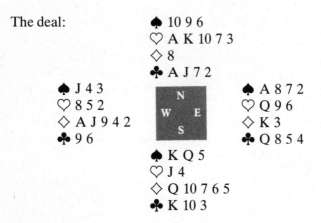

```
               ♠ 10 9 6
               ♡ A K 10 7 3
               ◇ 8
               ♣ A J 7 2
♠ J 4 3                        ♠ A 8 7 2
♡ 8 5 2          N            ♡ Q 9 6
◇ A J 9 4 2   W     E         ◇ K 3
♣ 9 6            S            ♣ Q 8 5 4
               ♠ K Q 5
               ♡ J 4
               ◇ Q 10 7 6 5
               ♣ K 10 3
```

Hand No. 59
Which diamond you play now does not matter—the hand is over.

The deal:

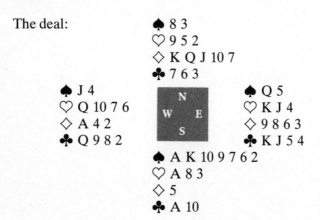

```
               ♠ 8 3
               ♡ 9 5 2
               ◇ K Q J 10 7
               ♣ 7 6 3
♠ J 4                          ♠ Q 5
♡ Q 10 7 6       N            ♡ K J 4
◇ A 4 2        W     E        ◇ 9 8 6 3
♣ Q 9 8 2        S            ♣ K J 5 4
               ♠ A K 10 9 7 6 2
               ♡ A 8 3
               ◇ 5
               ♣ A 10
```

Now, how did you follow to those trumps? With that diamond

140

suit on dummy, you should have realised that, if South has the ace, be it singleton or otherwise, there is nothing to discuss as the hand is now definitely off or definitely making irrespective of the defence. If West has the ace, however, the information he must have is your count in diamonds before the suit is played.

The Lone Ranger comes to the rescue. You should have played the queen followed by the five to show an even number of diamonds. West would then have realised that, if South has a trebleton, he has a good fit and must surely make the contract. He thus plays South for a singleton winning first time.

South's alternative line of play, possibly better, is to try the diamond at trick two. In that case, West has to take a view but will probably go up and now you must give the count. If you show a trebleton West will play another diamond immediately conceding two tricks instead of one but that may not be fatal.

Hand No. 60

The first point you should have remarked on was the order in which your partner cashed his three diamond winners. He was trying to indicate holdings in both or neither of the other two suits. As you have picked up your usual power house, you will have to hope that it is both. That means that partner will have discard problems on the run of the spades. The easiest way to give the count in hearts is the Bechgaard echo 4 3 2 or the like. West can now roll-call South to a singleton and abandon the suit, keeping his clubs for the setting trick. You should have played the ten at some stage when following the diamonds e.g. 5 2 10 to indicate a feature in hearts:

The deal:

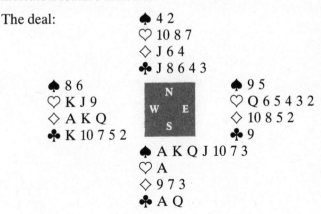

```
                  ♠ 4 2
                  ♡ 10 8 7
                  ◇ J 6 4
                  ♣ J 8 6 4 3
♠ 8 6                          ♠ 9 5
♡ K J 9          N             ♡ Q 6 5 4 3 2
◇ A K Q      W       E         ◇ 10 8 5 2
♣ K 10 7 5 2     S             ♣ 9
                  ♠ A K Q J 10 7 3
                  ♡ A
                  ◇ 9 7 3
                  ♣ A Q
```

Perhaps you are now convinced that bad cards are not as uninteresting as they might appear and that there is scope for considerable skill in handling them. Many unmakable contracts are presented to declarer through defenders with poor cards losing interest and following suit or discarding carelessly. This is one of the reasons overbidders continue to thrive. With industry and careful discussion and practice with your partner, you can become a stronger defender and, at least against you, they might control their tongues!